POPULAR DAY HIKES

Canadian Rockies

TONY DAFFERN

T0160369

RMB

Copyright © 2019 by Tony Daffern
First Revised and Updated Edition
Originally published in 2007 as *Popular Day Hikes 2: Canadian Rockies*

For information on purchasing bulk quantities of this book, or to obtain media excerpts or invite the author to speak at an event, please visit rmbooks.com and select the "Contact" tab.

RMB | Rocky Mountain Books Ltd.
rmbooks.com
@rmbooks
facebook.com/rmbooks

Cataloguing data available from Library and Archives Canada
ISBN 9781771602679 (paperback)
ISBN 9781771602686 (electronic)

Printed and bound in Canada by Friesens

We would like to also take this opportunity to acknowledge the traditional territories upon which we live and work. In Calgary, Alberta, we acknowledge the Niitsitapi (Blackfoot) and the people of the Treaty 7 region in Southern Alberta, which includes the Siksika, the Piikuni, the Kainai, the Tsuut'ina and the Stoney Nakoda First Nations, including Chiniki, Bearpaw, and Wesley First Nations. The City of Calgary is also home to Métis Nation of Alberta, Region III. In Victoria, British Columbia, we acknowledge the traditional territories of the Lkwungen (Esquimalt, and Songhees), Malahat, Pacheedaht, Scia'new, T'Sou-ke and W̱SÁNEĆ (Pauquachin, Tsartlip, Tsawout, Tseycum) peoples.

We acknowledge the financial support of the Government of Canada through the Canada Book Fund and the Canada Council for the Arts, and of the province of British Columbia through the British Columbia Arts Council and the Book Publishing Tax Credit.

Disclaimer

There are inherent risks in hiking mountain areas that require hikers to constantly use their own judgement. Anyone using this book does so entirely at their own risk and both the author and publisher disclaim any liability for any injuries or other damage that may be sustained by anyone hiking any of the trails described in this book.

Be aware that bear sightings and fire hazard can close trails at a moment's notice. Flash floods can wash out bridges. Fallen trees resulting from strong chinook winds can block trails and make the going difficult.

In this book there are no dos and don'ts. It is assumed that users are caring, intelligent people who will respect the country they are travelling through and its wildlife.

Contents

Area Map

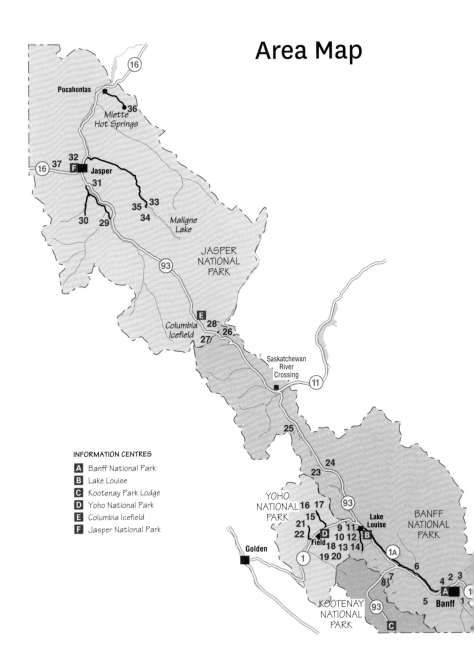

Pocahontas

36
Miette Hot Springs

16
37
32
F
Jasper
31
35 33
34
30 29
Maligne Lake

JASPER NATIONAL PARK

93

Columbia Icefield
E
28 26
27

Saskatchewan River Crossing
11

25

24
23

YOHO NATIONAL PARK
16 17
15
21
22
D
Field
9 11
10 12
18 13 14
19 20

93
Lake Louise
B
BANFF NATIONAL PARK

1A
6

Golden
1

7
8
4 2 3
A
5 Banff
1

KOOTENAY NATIONAL PARK
93
C

INFORMATION CENTRES
A Banff National Park
B Lake Louise
C Kootenay Park Lodge
D Yoho National Park
E Columbia Icefield
F Jasper National Park

Introduction

Hiking in the Canadian Rockies

The Canadian Rockies is an area of high limestone peaks (up to 3954 m), glaciers, waterfalls, blue-green lakes, boisterous streams and forested valley bottoms of spruce and fir with larches at treeline.

Alpine meadows are the reward for hiking up through sometimes dense forest. For too brief a time, from early July to mid-August, they are crammed with flowers. In particular, overseas visitors will be intoxicated by the gaudy colours of North America's Indian paintbrush. I advise all flower buffs to buy a field guide to put in their pack.

Getting to the trailhead

See the map on page 4. Other than a few buses that run along the Trans-Canada Highway and from Banff to Jasper, there is no public transportation. I have included one trail in both Banff and Jasper where you can walk or ride town transit to the trailhead. You can also walk up to the lake if you are staying in Lake Louise Village. For all other trails, you need a car.

Weather

The higher-elevation trails of the Canadian Rockies enjoy a very short hiking season. Winter snowfall can be heavy, so many trails are not completely clear of snow until mid-July. Hiking usually starts in mid-May on lower-elevation trails. In May there is usually a period of warm, sunny weather. Rains fall mainly in June–the peak runoff time. During July and August temperatures can reach the mid-30s and there may be late afternoon thunderstorms. However, snow can fall in any month of the year and conditions at higher elevations can be really foul. The weather starts cooling off in mid-September. Indian summers can occur in late September through October and are glorious, bringing sunny, stable weather. By the end of October, there is usually too much snow at higher elevations for hiking.

Drinking water

Most locals drink from the creeks. However, there is a chance the water, especially at lower elevations, may be contaminated by *Giardia lamblia*, a parasite that can cause severe gastrointestinal distress. It is best to carry water from your home, hotel or campground.

Wildlife concerns

It is unlikely that you will encounter bears if you are hiking these popular trails during normal daytime hiking hours. Having said that, you should constantly be alert for signs of bears (tracks, scat), particularly in early fall when the berries ripen. Parks Canada will often close a trail until a bear has moved out of the area. See the Group Access information for the Moraine Lake Area on page 53, which requires hikers to travel in tight groups of four. Make a lot of noise if you suspect there is a bear in the area.

Elk and moose should also be given a wide berth, especially in fall during the mating season, when males get very ornery. Lately, cougars have become a year-round worry. However, they are rarely seen, as are wolves. Be wary of picas, ground squirrels and chipmunks. They bite and could carry disease.

Dogs in Jasper National Park

Dogs are not allowed on trails in Jasper National Park in important caribou habitat, in order to reduce stress on this threatened species. Dogs are not allowed on any of the trails in the Maligne Lake area nor at Cavell Meadows.

Lake O'Hara

Lake O'Hara is only accessible by pre-booking a bus or by hiking 11 km up the access trail. The bus service runs from mid-June to the end of September. The first bus leaves at 8:30 in the morning and the last bus out is at 6:30 in the evening—ample time for a good day's hiking. For reservation information go to www.reservation.parkscanada.gc.ca. Be sure to arrive early. Bus reservations become invalid 10 minutes before departure time and may be given away.

In order to fully appreciate this beautiful area you may choose to use one of the two accommodation options available to those who have not booked in at the Lodge a long time in advance.

Camping

Campground reservations may be made up to three months in advance by calling Parks Canada at 250-343-6433. Your campground reservation also secures you a place on the bus. Visit the Parks Canada web site mentioned above for more information.

Elizabeth Parker Hut

You can stay at the Alpine Club of Canada's Elizabeth Parker Hut if space is available. Call 403-678-3200 for reservations. Your reservation also secures you a place on the bus. Before you consider this option, be sure to visit www.alpineclubofcanada.ca. Follow the links Huts > Booking Huts.

Le Relais day shelter

Operated by the Lake O'Hara Trails Club, this small concession provides trail information, hot drinks and snacks (cash only).

Bus schedule

To O'Hara 8:30, 10:30 a.m. and 3:30, 5:30 p.m. From O'Hara 9:30, 11:30 a.m. and 2:30, 4:30, 6:30 p.m.

Sunshine Meadows

Access to Sunshine Meadows is via gondola or shuttle bus. The gondola operates Fri to Mon inclusive during July and August. The shuttle bus is available Tue to Thu in July and August and 7 days a week during the first 3 weeks of September. No pets. At other times you will have to walk up the access road.

The gondola and shuttle bus leave from Sunshine Village parking lot from 8 am to 6 pm. Last bus down is 5:45 p.m. Fares in 2018: gondola $42 adults, $21 children 6-15; bus $35 adults, $19 children.

Reservations are recommended, but not required. Visit banffsunshinemeadows .com for more information and to make a reservation, or phone 1-877-542-2633.

There are also several buses a day from and back to Banff. The service is complementary with a gondola or shuttle reservation. You can reserve online or buy tickets on the bus. Check online for times and pickup points.

Lake Louise and Moraine Lake

Parking at Lake Louise and Moraine Lake is getting very difficult. Spaces are filling up by 6:00 am and Parks Canada is struggling to deal with the large influx of visitors. Various schemes are being tried (2018) such as public transit from Banff and shuttle buses from the Lake Louise overflow area east of the village on the Trans-Canada Highway.

If you want to do any of the hikes that start from Lake Louise or Moraine Lake it is absolutely essential that you phone or stop in at the Lake Louise visitor centre, or contact Parks Canada for the latest access information. See page 144 for contact details.

Using this Book

How the trails were chosen

For their popularity, first of all. You are not likely to be alone. They are easily accessible from a road, start from parking lots that usually have biffies and picnic tables and are generally well marked. To give variety they range from short to long and from easy walks to scrambles.

Trails

In this book most of the trails are obvious and have signposts at junctions. Above treeline watch for cairns or paint splodges on rocks. A few of the lower-elevation trails near Banff or Jasper are shared with mountain bikers and equestrians.

Options

Type in blue indicates Going Farther, Alternatives and Optional Returns.

Hazard or regulations

Occasional red type is used to convey a warning either of hazard or of a regulation that must be followed.

Numbers in text

For clarity the text is written in short, numbered paragraphs. Numbers in the photo captions refer back to the related paragraph numbers. Numbers in photo captions with an O in front of them refer to the option.

Difficulty

This describes conditions underfoot and the steepness of the grades. Scramble steps are noted. A few of the Going Farthers involve scrambling or going off trail.

Except after rain or during runoff, minor creeks can usually be jumped or crossed on rocks. All major creeks are bridged.

Distances

Distances are round trip, car to car, from the exit of the parking lot to the end of the trail as described in this guide.

Height gain

Height gains in this guide are total height gains for the round trip and include any significant height gained on the return.

Sketch maps

Red lines indicate main trails. Red-dashed lines are options. Black-dashed lines are other trails and are generally only shown where they intersect the red trails. Distances and positions of red lines were obtained using GPS track logs. Black-dashed lines are not guaranteed to be accurate. North is at the top of all maps. Contour interval is 100 m.

Do I need other maps?

Providing you stay on the trail it's possible to hike these routes using the maps in this book. Gem Trek publishes maps that cover all of the trails here, but you need to buy a lot of maps to cover them. Gem Trek maps are available at most outdoors stores, bookstores and gas stations in the region.

What to wear for the trails

Be prepared for fast weather changes, and pack raingear. For walks and scrambles above treeline take a wind jacket, long pants and extra warm clothing. During the summer a sun hat, sun cream and mosquito repellent are must-takes. Light hiking boots suffice for all the trails in this book. Heavier boots are to be preferred on some of the scrambling options.

Doing more

If you have enjoyed the trails in this book and wish to hike in other areas of the Canadian Rockies, consider Kananaskis Country, located south and west of Calgary in the eastern foothills of the Rockies.

A companion to this book, *Popular Day Hikes: Kananaskis Country* by Gillean Daffern, features 38 hikes throughout Kananaskis Country.

1 Spray River Loop

A pleasant walk with views of the Spray River and the long ridge of Mount Rundle. This is the only day hike in the Banff area that can be accessed via public transportation.

DISTANCE: 11.5 km loop

HEIGHT GAIN: 120 m

HIGH POINT: 1460 m

MODERATE

YEAR-ROUND

START: Cross the bridge over the Bow River at the south end of Banff Avenue. Turn left. Keep left at the next traffic light and drive to the Banff Springs Hotel. Keep right around the traffic circle and pass under the bridge. Follow the road, bearing to the right past the staff parking, to its end at Spray River trailhead parking.

If you are in Banff without your own transportation you can ride the Banff public transit bus to the Banff Springs Hotel. Check with your hotel or the information centre for routes and schedules.

DIFFICULTY: An easy trail following old fire roads that you will be sharing with mountain bikers. In winter it is groomed and trackset with the tracks on either side, leaving space for you to walk in the middle. It can get very icy, so hiking poles are in order.

1. Follow the wide trail on the west side of the Spray River through spruce and pine forest to a trail junction at 700 m. The trail to the left leads down to the river and will be your return route.

2. Keep straight ahead for now. Just after the top of the first climb look for a horse trail to the left. It makes a pleasant alternative to the fire road for the next kilometre.

At a junction near the river, keep right and climb back up to the fire road.

3. The road finally descends, and the forest opens up to allow views of the river and the long ridge of Mount Rundle to your left. Arrive at a junction and picnic area. The trail straight ahead continues up the Spray River valley (see option).

4. Turn left toward the river and descend a few feet to the bridge. Beyond the bridge the trail climbs gently for the next three kilometres, passing Mount Rundle campsite after about half a kilometre.

5. Keep your eyes open for a trail sign on your left indicating the start of Old Quarry Loop.

6. Turn left and follow the trail as it traverses down across a steep bank toward the river. You can see the bridge downstream

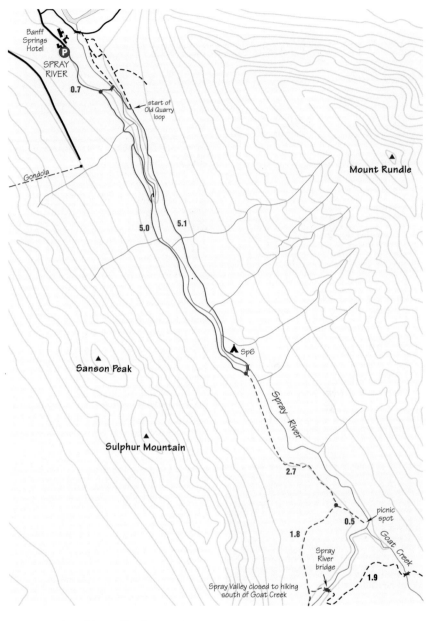

Banff
Springs
Hotel

SPRAY RIVER

0.7

start of Old Quarry loop

Gondola

Mount Rundle

5.0   5.1

Sanson Peak

Sp6

Spray River

Sulphur Mountain

2.7

picnic spot

0.5

Goat Creek

1.8

Spray River bridge

1.9

Spray Valley closed to hiking south of Goat Creek

OPPOSITE: *View of the Banff Springs Hotel from the top of the bank near the start of Old Quarry Loop (5).*

that you will be crossing shortly. A couple of switchbacks bring you down to river level where the trail follows the river edge to the bridge.

7. Cross the bridge and climb the bank to the trail junction mentioned in 1. Turn right to return to the trailhead.

TOP: *The bridge over the Spray River (4).*

BOTTOM: *Mount Rundle from the Spray River Bridge at O2.*

Going farther up the Spray Valley

DISTANCE: add 6.4 km to picnic spot, 9 km to Spray River bridge and about 120 m height gain.

You can wander farther up the Spray Valley into Kananaskis Country. However, a logical turnaround point is the bridge over the Spray River. The Spray Valley beyond Goat Creek has been closed to travel in recent years as a result of the park's bear management program.

1. At the end of 3, continue straight ahead, following the gradually ascending Spray Valley for 2.7 km to an obvious junction on the left.

2. Here you have the option of turning left and descending to a picnic spot by the river or carrying straight on to the bridge over the Spray River. If the latter, keep left at a junction where your trail leaves the main Spray Valley fire road.

3. Return the way you came, turning right across the river when you regain the main loop at (4).

2 Cascade Amphitheatre

A demanding trail to an impressive amphitheatre tucked into the west side of Cascade Mountain. Alpine wildflowers, pikas, hoary marmots and occasional mountain goats are the attractions here.

DISTANCE: 15 km return

HEIGHT GAIN: 640 m

HIGH POINT: 2195 m

MODERATELY STRENUOUS

JULY TO MID-SEPTEMBER

START: Follow the Mount Norquay road from the Banff west interchange to Ski Norquay ski area. Park at the far end of the large parking lot.

DIFFICULTY: Easy downhill to start with, following a ski area access road and then a good trail to Forty Mile Creek. After crossing the creek there is a steady uphill climb with steep zigzags for the last 2 km to the amphitheatre. On the return there is a 155 m climb back up to the ski area.

1. From the parking lot walk between the day lodge and service buildings and follow the gravel road past Cascade Chair for 1.2 km to Mystic Chair. Ignore a hiking sign just before Spirit Chair. The overgrown trail it indicates does not save height gain or distance.

2. The trail to Forty Mile Creek starts a few metres beyond the chairlift. After a short uphill, head steadily downhill to a junction. Trail to Mystic Lake to left. Keep right and continue downhill to Forty Mile Creek. Turn left across the bridge onto Elk Lakes trail.

3. Climb steadily for 1.5 km to another junction. The trail to Elk Lakes heads off left. Bear right for the Cascade Amphitheatre.

Cascade Amphitheatre from the summit ridge of Cascade Mountain.

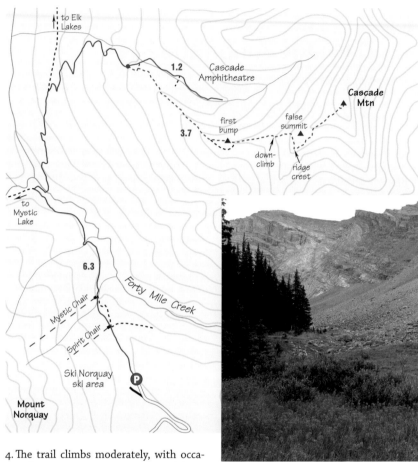

to Elk Lakes

1.2 Cascade Amphitheatre

Cascade Mtn

first bump

3.7

false summit

down-climb

ridge crest

to Mystic Lake

6.3

Forty Mile Creek

Mystic Chair

Spirit Chair

Ski Norquay ski area

P

Mount Norquay

4. The trail climbs moderately, with occasional steep sections, in a series of large switchbacks through thick forest until it suddenly flattens out at the start of the amphitheatre.

5. The trail continues through subalpine forest and flower meadows to the head of the amphitheatre just beyond the last trees and by a tiny creek. Trails to the right are climber's trails for the ascent of Cascade Mountain.

6. Return the way you came.

TOP: *A much foreshortened view of the summit of Cascade Mountain from near the last trees. The False Summit is seen in profile to the right.*

BOTTOM: *This golden-mantled ground squirrel appeared within a few minutes of my sitting down by the tiny creek near the head of the cirque.*

Option: Cascade Mountain

HEIGHT GAIN: 820 m from amphitheatre

HIGH POINT: 2998 m

From the amphitheatre, the right-hand ridge appears an obvious and easy way to the summit. It is, however, a moderately difficult scramble and a much more serious undertaking than hiking the trail. It involves loose scree and talus and potentially tricky route-finding. It should only be attempted by experienced scramblers.

If you think you will be tempted to make the ascent once at the amphitheatre, you should request a copy of the excellent pamphlet "A Climber's Guide to Cascade Mountain" from the information centre in Banff.

The climb should only be attempted in good weather and after the winter snow has melted. Check the left skyline ridge as viewed from Banff Avenue for snow before you make a decision. It is usually clear of snow by early to mid-July.

1. There are several trails accessing the ridge. The most straightforward is a narrow trail to the right as soon as the main trail levels out to enter the amphitheatre. Follow this uphill for about 150 m to a junction. Turn right. Straight on leads back to the main trail. Climb steeply onto the ridge.

2. Continue up the rocky ridge, which is treed to start with, and over the first bump on an easy dirt trail and over rocks. Don't follow a tempting cairned route to the right. Stick to the ridge, scrambling down the far side of the first bump. From here, start to look behind you frequently so as to memorize the route for your descent.

3. Continue up zigzags on grass and rock until you reach a section of moderately steep rock slabs at the edge of a cliffband. Scramble down a couple of metres to the right and continue just below the ridgeline. This descent is the key to accessing the traverse line to the right across the slopes of the False Summit. Note the descent location for your return.

4. Continue upward, watching for another short downclimb that allows you to access the start of the False Summit traverse. Follow the good (except for a couple of smooth, gritty slabs) trail that leads right for 150 m to the right-hand skyline. Note where the trail reaches the ridge for your descent.

5. Scramble down a couple of metres and climb loose scree up along the base of the cliff to a ridge at the edge of a steep bowl. Cross the steep, exposed bowl on a good, though narrow, trail to the main ridge beyond the False Summit. This section is potentially very dangerous when snow covered—consider turning back.

6. Follow the ridge up steep, loose talus to the top.

7. Descend exactly the same way as you came up. Do not attempt any shortcuts however tempting. Take your time—it is easy to get off route, with potentially serious consequences. There are three places that require particular route-finding attention.

8. Make sure you locate the top of the False Summit traverse line (4). It is at the highest point at which it is possible to cross the ridge, and the traverse is immediately visible when you scramble onto the ridge. Do not follow a false trail that leads to a small saddle lower down.

9. Take time to locate the route up the cliffband to the foot of the slabs mentioned in (3).

10. After descending the ridge from the slabs, scramble up to the top of the first bump and descend the ridge. There is an inviting traverse trail to the left, but this route necessitates a long rightward traverse across loose boulders to regain the ascent ridge. See the black-dashed line on the map.

11. Continue down the ridge to the main amphitheatre trail.

TOP: *The summit side of the first bump. It is best to traverse directly over the bump on both ascent and descent. The well-used trail to the left requires a long traverse back to the ridge above the amphitheatre, which swings to the right. The trail to the left could lead you significantly off route when visibility is bad.*

MIDDLE: *This photo shows the route described in O3&4. It is the key to a trouble-free ascent.*

LEFT: *The traverse around the False Summit (O4).*

LEFT: *The back side of the False Summit. There is a big drop-off at bottom left so be prepared to back off if the slope is snow covered.*

MIDDLE LEFT: *A foreshortened view of the summit ridge from the back of the False Summit.*

MIDDLE RIGHT: *This mountain goat appeared around the rock on the right in the photo below just a few seconds after I had taken the picture—startling us both.*

BOTTOM: *Lake Minnewanka from the summit. The prominent peaks across the lake are Mount Inglismaldie (left) and Mount Girouard.*

3 C-Level Cirque

A classic scree- and boulder-strewn Canadian Rockies cirque carved into the cliffs of Cascade Mountain.

DISTANCE: 9.4 km return

HEIGHT GAIN: 455 m

HIGH POINT: 1920 m

MODERATELY STRENUOUS

MID-JUNE TO END OF SEPTEMBER

START: Follow the Lake Minnewanka road from the Banff east interchange for 3.5 km and turn left into the Upper Bankhead picnic site. The trail starts at the far west (left as you drive in) corner of the parking lot.

DIFFICULTY: A good, moderately steep trail all the way.

1. The trail follows an old mine access track through the forest to the old C-Level shaft, passing the remains of an old mine building on the way.

2. From the building a trail to the right climbs up onto the tailings pile to a viewpoint offering good views of Lake Minnewanka backdropped by the Fairholme Range and the Bow Valley with Mount Rundle in the background.

3. The trail continues climbing past old, fenced-off mine workings (take either trail at a fork), then enters dense forest that persists until shortly before you reach the rocky knoll at the entrance to the cirque.

Old mine building a short way up the trail. A trail to the right leads to a tailings pile with good views.

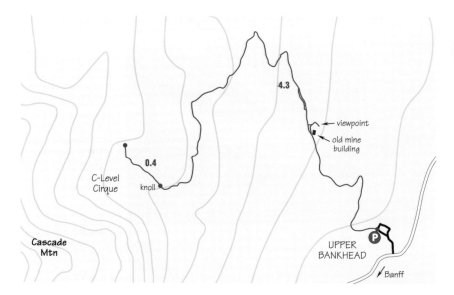

4. Descend slightly to the right and follow a narrow, moderately steep trail to a rocky bench. Large boulders provide good seating while you admire the view.

5. Return the way you came.

Note: It is possible, but not recommended, to scramble through trees and up scree at the right-hand edge of the cirque until high enough for good views of Lake Minnewanka and the Bow Valley.

The upper slopes of the cirque are still snowbound in mid-June.

TOP: *Starting the descent from the rocky bench (4).*

MIDDLE: *Looking down from the upper trail toward the rocky knoll (3).*

BOTTOM: *Lake Minnewanka from the right-hand edge of the cirque. Mount Inglismaldie reaching into the cloud at centre right.*

4 Cory Pass–Edith Pass Circuit

The premier hike in the Banff area takes you across a high pass, under the nearly vertical southeast face of Mount Louis and around the rocky pinnacles of Mount Edith.

DISTANCE: 13.7 km loop

HEIGHT GAIN: 1035 m

HIGH POINT: 2350 m

VERY STRENUOUS

MID-JULY TO MID-SEPTEMBER

START: Drive west from Banff on the Trans-Canada Highway. Turn right onto the 1A Parkway 5.7 km west of the Norquay interchange. After 300 m turn right and follow the road to its end at the Fireside Picnic Area.

DIFFICULTY: An arduous, leg-numbing 925 m ascent to Cory Pass in one direction or a toe-jamming descent if you hike the circuit in the other direction. Some prefer to get the hard part over early in the day. Photographers prefer the anticlockwise direction to get the best light on the mountains. Whichever direction you choose, it is an outing for tough, experienced hikers.

Clockwise

1. From the trailhead, cross the creek, turn right and follow an old road 300 m downhill. Turn left onto a good trail and proceed to the Cory Pass/Edith Pass trail junction. To hike the circuit clockwise (Cory Pass first) turn left; otherwise go straight on.

2. The trail begins a long, steep uphill climb on an open, south-facing slope—a good reason to start early—then switchbacks through trees onto the end of Mount Edith's south ridge.

3. Continue easily along the ridge through trees with views ahead of Mount Edith and Cory Pass. A short uphill precedes a downhill scramble to a small col between the ridge and Mount Edith. The rock is polished and care must be taken.

4. From the base of the rock step follow the trail up the ridge through trees a short way before embarking on a long, rising traverse to Cory pass across generally open slopes. The trail is sometimes sketchy where it crosses shale gullies. Ignore a climber's trail to the right. Arrive at the pass, a rocky defile with a good view of Mount Edith.

5. After a well-deserved rest, descend the steep talus slope on the north side of the pass. A little way down you get the first view of the impressive southeast face of Mount Louis. After the initial steep descent the grade eases off on a long, descending traverse to the right on scree slopes above Gargoyle Valley. Arrive at a jumble of boulders at the narrowest part of the valley between the sheer faces of mounts Edith and Louis.

6. From here pick your way down the rocky defile, following cairns traversing rightward on scree to the start of the 60 m climb around Edith's north ridge. Climb across a scree slope, taking a right-hand option low down. Continue into trees—sign—and climb through forest to a high point. Note a climber's trail to the right. Carry straight on, making a descending traverse across avalanche slopes on the northeast slope of Mount Edith. A steeper descent through ever-increasing trees brings you to the environs of forested Edith Pass.

7. Continue down through trees to the main Edith Pass trail. To the left is the trail to Forty Mile Creek. Turn right.

8. Continue down the shady valley through mossy forest following the line of the stream for 3 km to a point close to the highway. Here the trail turns right, crosses Edith Creek and ascends a short hill to the Cory Pass/Edith Pass trail junction and the completion of the circuit. Carry straight on to the trailhead in 1.2 km.

TOP LEFT: *The partially forested slopes below Mount Edith leading to Cory Pass.*

TOP RIGHT: *The sometimes sketchy trail in the last kilometre before the pass.*

BOTTOM LEFT: *The southeast face of Mount Louis from just below Cory Pass. Climbers descend to the col on the left, then pick their way down steep slopes to Gargoyle Valley.*

BOTTOM RIGHT: *The short downhill scramble mentioned in 3.*

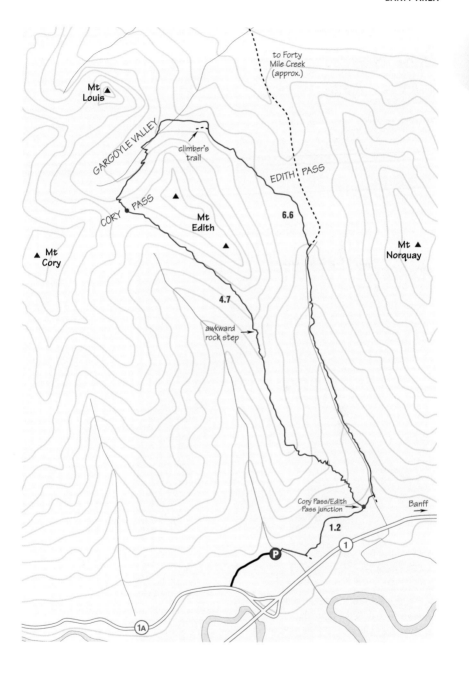

TOP: *The trail stays high above the right-hand side of Gargoyle Valley until it descends to a jumble of boulders below the north buttress of Mount Edith.*

LEFT: *Mount Louis from the scree slope at the start of the climb around Mount Edith's north ridge (6).*

5 Sunshine Meadows

Flower-filled subalpine meadows with unobstructed views, deep blue lakes, picturesque islets and a distant view of Mount Assiniboine.

DISTANCE: 11.3 km loop

HEIGHT GAIN: 160 m

HIGH POINT: 2305 m

MODERATE

GONDOLA OR BUS JULY AND AUGUST

START: From Banff head west on the Trans-Canada Hwy. for 8 km and turn off at the Sunshine Village exit. Follow the road 7 km to the far end of the large parking lot. The ticket office is on the lower floor of the building on the left and opens at 8:00 a.m. daily.

SUNSHINE MEADOWS GONDOLA & SHUTTLE

See page 6 for information.

At the village there is a small deli where you can purchase drinks and snacks.

DIFFICULTY: Good, well-maintained trails suitable for all ages.

1. Follow a wide gravel track uphill from the centre of the village. Turn left just past the Avalanche Control log cabin (signed).

2. The trail climbs steadily uphill through the ski area meadows to the Great Divide—the boundary between Alberta and British Columbia. Ignore a trail to the left that goes to the base of a chairlift. Arrive at a junction. The trail to the left goes to Citadel Pass about 8 km away. Keep right to Rock Isle Lake.

3. You soon reach the Rock Isle Lake viewpoint. Carry on around the lake, noting two trails to the right to Twin Cairns. Keep left and descend to Rock Isle Lake's outlet stream. From here you can see Grizzly and Larix lakes below. Descend to a junction marking the start of a loop around the two lakes. You can go either way. Don't miss the Simpson Viewpoint.

4. Having completed the loop, head back up to Rock Isle Lake to the previously noted Twin Cairns junction. If you turn right you will return directly to Sunshine Village but miss out on a great viewpoint. Turn left.

5. The trail heads toward the valley between Twin Cairns and Standish Ridge. At the next junction turn right and climb fairly steeply to

Summer wildflowers.

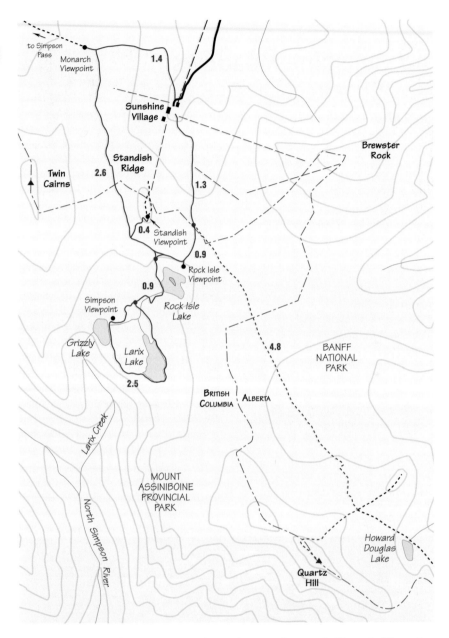

Standish Viewpoint, where you are treated to expansive views of the Sunshine meadows.

6. Return to the junction with Twin Cairns trail and turn right. Follow the trail through flower meadows to the junction with the Simpson Pass trail. Monarch Viewpoint, with a view of Mount Ball, is about 200 m to the left. Turn right and return to Sunshine Village.

TOP: *Rock Isle Lake. The sharply pointed peak in the centre distance is part of Split Peak in Kootenay National Park.*

MIDDLE: *Rock Isle and Larix lakes from Standish Viewpoint. Mount Assiniboine is just visible between the summits of Quartz Hill.*

BOTTOM: *Larix Lake backdropped by the imposing wall of The Monarch.*

TOP: *Hiking the trail between Standish Ridge and Twin Cairns. Standish Viewpoint is up the hill at the top left of the picture.*

MIDDLE LEFT: *White and yellow daisies.*

MIDDLE RIGHT: *The unusually dark-red Indian paintbrush common in Sunshine Meadows.*

BOTTOM: *A well-camouflaged ptarmigan among the quartz rocks on the lower summit of Quartz Hill.*

Option: Quartz Hill

DISTANCE: 12.2 km return from Sunshine

HEIGHT GAIN: 195 m

If you want more of a wilderness experience than the often crowded hike to Rock Isle, Grizzly and Larix lakes, you can follow the Citadel Pass trail to the broad northeast ridge of Quartz Hill, then scramble to the top.

1. Turn left at the Rock Isle Lake–Citadel Pass junction (2) onto the Citadel Pass trail. The wider trail to the right goes to the lakes.

2. Head southeast across open, flower-filled meadows. Descend slightly into a basin with occasional stands of larches, then climb steeply through heavier tree cover to the broad ridge. If you don't feel like scrambling to the top of Quartz Hill you can turn left here and enjoy the views from the end of the ridge.

3. From the ridge crest turn right and head straight up the ridge, keeping to the rocky areas as much as possible, to the foot of Quartz Hill. Climb directly up to the first group of rocks, then make a moderately steep, rising traverse to the right on grass and then scree, to the rocky northwest ridge. Scramble up the ridge to the twin summits and a magnificent 360° view.

4. Return the way you came.

LEFT: *Heading along the northeast ridge toward the higher summit of Quartz Hill (O3).*

BOTTOM: *The higher peak of Quartz Hill has two small summits. Mount Assiniboine towers in the background.*

6 Johnston Canyon to Inkpots

A spectacular canyon with multiple waterfalls, tufa deposits, black swifts and dippers. Continue to five quicksand-bottomed mineral ponds fed by karst springs.

DISTANCE: 12.2 km return

HEIGHT GAIN: 445 m

HIGH POINT: 1760 m

MODERATE

JUNE TO OCTOBER: middle to end of June is best for waterfalls.

START: Drive west from Banff on the Trans-Canada Highway. Turn right onto the 1A Parkway 5.5 km west of the Norquay interchange. After 17.8 km turn right into a parking lot signed "Johnston Canyon" about 200 m before the Johnston Canyon Resort. From Lake Louise, drive toward Banff on either Hwy. 1 or 1A. The resort is 6.5 km east of Castle Junction. The trail starts at the far west corner of the parking lot.

DIFFICULTY: A broad, paved trail with catwalks and viewpoints through the canyon followed by a good trail to the Inkpots.

1. A short trail crosses Johnston Creek to the resort. Turn right and follow the paved trail through the canyon enjoying the splendour and power of rushing water and roaring cascades. If you have not been here before it's worth it in spite of the crowds.

2. Continue beyond the upper falls, leaving the crowds behind, to a junction. Turn right onto an old fire road.

3. Continue climbing to the high point of the trail, then descend 115 m to meadows and the Inkpots to the right.

4. Return the way you came. If you wish to avoid the crowds in the canyon, keep right where you previously joined the fire road (2). Watch for a signed hiking trail to Moose Meadows to the right. Keep straight on down the fire road, ignoring any side trails. Follow the track along the back of the resort and round into the resort parking lot. Cross the bridge to your stating point.

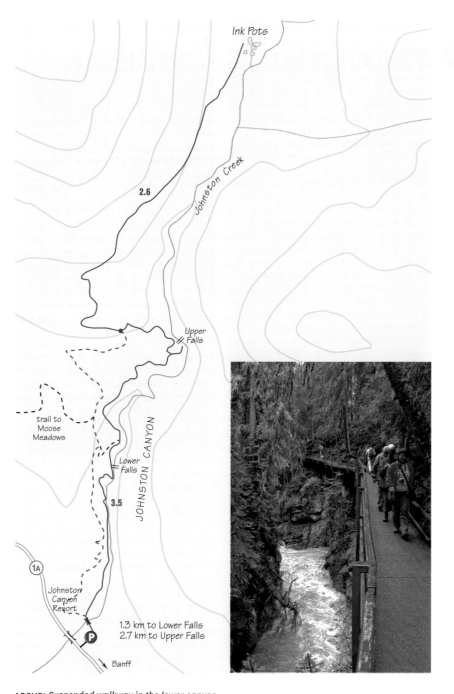

Ink Pots

Johnston Creek

2.6

Upper Falls

trail to Moose Meadows

Lower Falls

JOHNSTON CANYON

3.5

1A

Johnston Canyon Resort

P

Banff

1.3 km to Lower Falls
2.7 km to Upper Falls

ABOVE: *Suspended walkway in the lower canyon.*

OPPOSITE: *Boardwalks provide the only access to the deep, narrow early sections of the canyon.*

TOP LEFT: *The upper falls under normal runoff conditions.*

TOP RIGHT: *The lower falls during a period of high runoff. Cross the bridge to view the falls through the tunnel on the other side. Photographers: note that direct sunlight only reaches into the canyon for a couple of hours around midday—when it is most crowded.*

LEFT: *Spray from windblown water droplets and focused rays of sunshine in the narrow canyon combine to create frequent rainbows such as this one across the top of the upper falls.*

TOP LEFT: *A colourful wall of tufa on the far side of the canyon.*

TOP RIGHT: *Spring water bubbles up through the gravel and sand to form the five pools. The colour of the pools depends on the amount of fine, silty material on the bottom. The water remains at a constant temperature of about 4°C throughout the year.*

BOTTOM: *Enjoying a sunny day at the Inkpots. The mountain in the background is unnamed.*

7 Arnica Lake

A tranquil blue-green lake set below steep cliffs.

DISTANCE: 10 km return

HEIGHT GAIN: 710 m

HIGH POINT: 2150 m

STRENUOUS

JUNE TO END OF SEPTEMBER

START: From Castle Junction on the Trans-Canada Hwy., follow Hwy. 93 south toward Radium to the unsigned Vista Lake Viewpoint, 8.2 km west of Castle Junction. The viewpoint parking is 1.2 km west of the Boom Lake trailhead. Be careful—there is no left-turn lane off the highway.

DIFFICULTY: A good, moderately steep trail that climbs relentlessly. There is a 120 m height gain from Vista Lake up to your vehicle at the end of the day.

1. Head down the narrow trail to Vista Lake and cross the bridge over the lake's outlet.

2. The trail now climbs relentlessly up the slopes of Storm Mountain through recent growth of lodgepole pine seeded after the 1968 fire. An open, lightly treed ridge gives good views to Castle Mountain and Mount Whymper. Pass into mature forest and arrive at a small tarn.

LEFT: *Vista Lake. Mount Whymper in the background.*

OPPOSITE TOP: *Heartleaf arnica, from which the lake gets its name.*

OPPOSITE BOTTOM: *Arnica Lake below the cliffs of Storm Mountain's northeast ridge.*

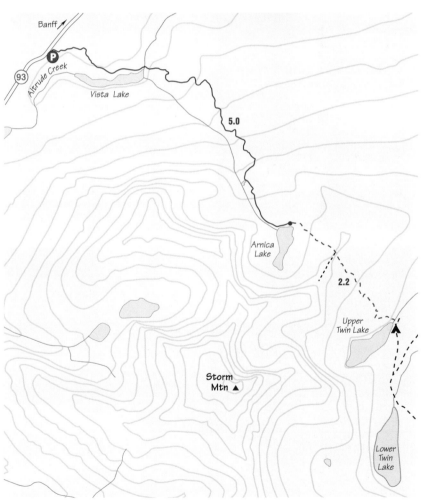

3. Sorry. This is not Arnica Lake. You still have 800 m and 80 m height gain to go. A short descent and you are at the lake.

4. Return the way you came.

Going farther to Upper Twin Lake

DISTANCE: add 4.4 km

HEIGHT GAIN: add 360 m

Extend your hike over a ridge to a larger, more colourful lake.

1. From Arnica Lake continue along the trail ascending 135 m to an attractive pass over a narrow, larch-forested ridge.

2. The trail now descends, steeply at first, to Upper Twin Lake, the more attractive of the two Twin Lakes. Cross the outlet creek on stepping stones to the campground.

3. Return the way you came.

TOP: *Crossing the stepping stones shortly before the backcountry campground at Upper Twin Lake.*

MIDDLE: *Upper Twin Lake from near the campground. Storm Mountain is up to the right.*

BOTTOM: *The pass between Arnica Lake and Upper Twin Lake in early summer. If you don't feel like going down to Twin Lake—and back up again—you can climb up the ridge to the right (southwest) until you get a good view across the Bow Valley to Castle Mountain.*

8 Stanley Glacier

From fire to ice. Brilliant flowers bloom against a background of burnt-black trees. A hanging valley with high peaks, a receding glacier and marmots.

DISTANCE: 9 km return

HEIGHT GAIN: 335 m

HIGH POINT: 1920 m

MODERATELY STRENUOUS

JUNE TO END OF SEPTEMBER

START: From Castle Junction on the Trans-Canada Hwy., follow Hwy. 93 south toward Radium to the Stanley Glacier parking area 3.5 km west of the Alberta–British Columbia boundary.

DIFFICULTY: Good, well-maintained trail with easy to moderate grades. Loose, rocky trail over talus moraines beyond the end of the official trail.

1. After crossing the bridge over the Vermilion River, the trail switchbacks steadily up through the burnt area into the side valley containing Stanley Glacier. Cross a bridge over Stanley Creek.

This area was devastated by fire in the 1968 Vermilion Pass burn. By the turn of the century the new forest had attained a height of about 8–10 metres. In 2003, in order to contain a massive fire to the west, this area was intentionally fired by Parks Canada. Note the blackened trees, still standing in 2007, and the larger charred deadfall from the earlier fire.

2. The grade soon eases as you follow the northeast side of the creek up the valley,

Approaching the end of the official trail. The triangular cliffband below the hanging valley is clearly visible in the centre of the picture.

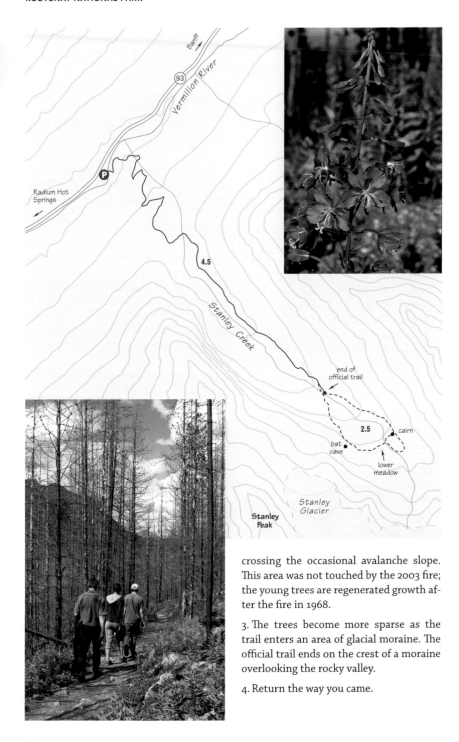

crossing the occasional avalanche slope. This area was not touched by the 2003 fire; the young trees are regenerated growth after the fire in 1968.

3. The trees become more sparse as the trail enters an area of glacial moraine. The official trail ends on the crest of a moraine overlooking the rocky valley.

4. Return the way you came.

Continue to a hanging valley

DISTANCE: add 2 km

HEIGHT GAIN: add 200 m

From the end of the official trail you can see trails on either side leading to a hanging valley above a triangular cliffband. The trail to the left is the easiest way up, leaving the steeper one to the right for the descent.

1. Continue up the rocky trail trending left onto the left-hand of the two trails heading for a treed slope. The one you want is immediately below the moraine on the left. Follow this moderately steep trail through the trees and across scree up to the left of the cliffs below the hanging valley. Arrive at a cairn at cliff-top level.

2. From the cairn you can cross the ridge to your right and descend to the lower meadow, or you can continue on the same line and make a circuit of the treed ridge, descending by the creek to the lower meadow. From here you have great views of the Stanley Glacier and back down the valley.

3. Either descend the way you came (easier) or head toward the west side of the valley on a good trail and descend below the cliffs (some exposure across a rock band), below the bat cave and down to the end of the official trail.

TOP: *Looking down on three different trails heading up toward the hanging valley from the end of the official trail. The upper trail, once you get on it, takes the best line up and across the slope.*

BOTTOM: *The bat cave is worth taking a look at. In winter, mixed rock and ice climbers hang bat-like from ice climbing tools protected by the many bolts leading out from the roof of the cave.*

OPPOSITE TOP: *Fireweed.*

OPPOSITE BOTTOM: *The trail passes through charred deadfall from the 1968 fire and scorched standing trees from the 2003 burn.*

9 Lake Agnes–Beehives Circuit

Impressive viewpoints, sheer cliffs, a blue-green lake in an enclosed cirque, and a teahouse. Chipmunks, pikas, marmots and ground squirrels.

DISTANCE: 13.7 km return
(Teahouse by shortest route 8.2 km)

HEIGHT GAIN: 670 m

HIGH POINT: 2255 m

MODERATELY STRENUOUS

YEAR ROUND TO LAKE AGNES, SUMMER AND FALL TO BIG BEEHIVE

START: From Lake Louise Village follow the well-signed road uphill to Lake Louise and park in the large public parking lot. Head toward the Chateau, cross the bridge over the outlet creek and follow the lakeside path in front of the Chateau to the far end.

DIFFICULTY: Good, well maintained trails that can be icy in winter. The switchbacks to Big Beehive provide a moderately angled route up a steep slope.

1. Fork right at a well-signed junction on the trail to Mirror Lake and Lake Agnes. Switchback up the broad, well-maintained trail, ignoring any junctions, to Mirror Lake. Turn right just before the lake.

2. Climb a few switchbacks to a junction where the trail to Little Beehive angles back to the right. Turn right.

3. After about 500 m note the trail heading back to the left. You will be following this trail to Lake Agnes on your return from Little Beehive. Pass the trail to Mount St. Piran on your left and climb to the crest of a ridge with views of both Lake Louise and Lake Agnes. Continue to Little Beehive viewpoint.

4. Retrace your steps past the Mount St. Piran junction to the aforementioned Lake Agnes connector trail, which reaches

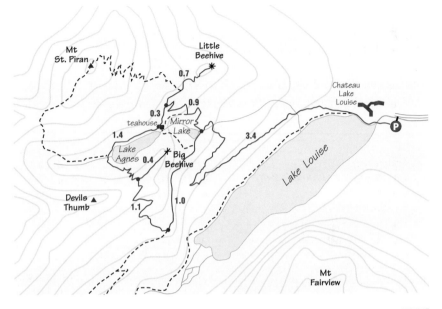

the lake just beyond the teahouse (open daily June to October from 10 to 6). They serve soup, sandwiches, cookies and pastries as well as many varieties of black and herbal teas.

5. After a stop for refreshment, follow the trail to the end of the lake. Note the switchbacks up the slope to the left as you go. They can be quite difficult to ascend if there is a lot of snow on them. This is the route to Big Beehive.

6. Boulder-hop across the creek at the end of the lake and embark on the switchbacks. Using a slow and steady "guides" pace you will soon reach the saddle between Lake Agnes and Lake Louise. Head left on a rocky trail for about 400 m to the gazebo at the Big Beehive viewpoint.

7. Retrace your steps to the saddle and turn left. The trail descends steeply in a few lazy zigzags to Highline Trail, which runs between Mirror Lake and the Plain of the Six Glaciers. Turn left and follow the trail through forest to Mirror Lake.

8. Return the way you came.

ABOVE: *Big Beehive from Mirror Lake.*

OPPOSITE: *Lake Agnes teahouse on a busy day at the end of June.*

TOP: *Looking down on the Chateau Lake Louise from just below Little Beehive viewpoint. The vista from here is better than at Little Beehive.*

LEFT: *Lake Agnes on a dull day from near the teahouse. Although it is the end of June, there is still a lot of snow around. The lower peak is Devils Thumb, with higher Mount Whyte on the right.*

TOP: *The switchback trail leading to Big Beehive still has some snow on it (5). It can be tricky earlier in the season when completely snow covered.*

MIDDLE: *The gazebo on the summit of Big Beehive is a good place to stop for a snack.*

BOTTOM: *Highline Trail descends gently to the Plain of the Six Glaciers trail, with outstanding views of The Mitre (off to the left), Mount Lefroy and Mount Victoria.*

Option: A two-teahouse day

If you are feeling energetic you can visit two teahouses in one day by turning right on Highline Trail (7) and following its scenic route with views of mounts Victoria and Lefroy as it gently traverses to the Plain of the Six Glaciers trail. Stay high at the next intersection for the best views. Return via the Lake Louise Lakeshore Trail. See hike #10, Plain of the Six Glaciers.

10 Plain of the Six Glaciers

A stark landscape of moraine, snow, ice and glacier-clad Mount Victoria.

DISTANCE: 14.8 km return

HEIGHT GAIN: 335 m

HIGH POINT: 2070 m

MODERATELY STRENUOUS

MID-JUNE TO END OF SEPTEMBER; YEAR-ROUND TO END OF LAKE

START: From Lake Louise Village follow the well-signed road uphill to Lake Louise and park in the large public lot. Head toward the Chateau, cross the bridge over the outlet creek and follow the lakeside path in front of the Chateau to the far end.

DIFFICULTY: Good, well-maintained trail, almost flat along the lake, then steady climbing to teahouse. Well-trodden, rocky moraine ending at a scree slope if you go farther.

1. Fork left at a well-signed junction and head around the lake on the scenic Lakeshore trail. Shortly after you pass the cliffs at the end of the lake the trail begins to climb steadily through open forest and across avalanche slopes, passing one junction with a shortcut trail leading to the Highline trail to Mirror Lake and another with the terminus of the Highline. See the option on page 43.

2. The trail emerges into an alpine world of rocky moraines. A little steeper now, it heads across ledges and open hillsides. Just as you get on the moraine, the trail divides. The upper trail traverses rock ledges with a cable handrail. If you don't have a head for heights, follow the lower trail. Make a few moderately steep switchbacks, then round a corner into a small patch of forest

containing the teahouse (open daily July to September from 10 a.m. to 4 p.m.). Here you can get soup, sandwiches, apple pie and a variety of teas.

3. The trail continues up the crest of a lateral moraine, gaining another 120 m of elevation from the teahouse to a viewpoint overlooking Victoria Glacier and the "Death Trap" couloir between mounts Lefroy and Victoria.

4. Return the way you came.

A more scenic option

DISTANCE: add 1.5 km and a little extra height gain.

Rather than hiking along the lakeshore each way, climb to Mirror Lake and follow scenic Highline Trail to the Plain of the Six Glaciers.

1. Fork right at the end of the Chateau on the trail to Lake Agnes. At Mirror Lake head left on Highline Trail. Keep straight on at all junctions, joining Lakeshore Trail just before it reaches the moraine.

2. On your return, follow Lakeshore Trail back to the Chateau.

TOP: *The upper and lower trails (2). If you don't have a head for heights, follow the lower trail.*

BOTTOM: *Plain of the Six Glaciers Teahouse.*

OPPOSITE: *The gentle trail along the lake. The quartzite cliff ahead is a popular rock-climbing crag.*

You will be sharing this trail with equestrians.

This red squirrel is used to hikers.

The final moraine ridge before the trail ends at the scree-slope viewpoint in the picture below (3). Lake Louise, with Fairview Mountain (hike #12, page 49) to its right, is visible in the distance.

Looking into the "Death Trap" between Mount Lefroy on the left and Mount Victoria. Because of the danger from falling seracs, the Abbot Pass climbers hut on the col is usually accessed from the Lake O'Hara side.

11 Mount St. Piran

Outstanding close-up views of rugged peaks and glaciers from one of the best hiker-accessible summits in the area.

DISTANCE: 13.4 km

HEIGHT GAIN: 915 m

HIGH POINT: 2649 m

STRENUOUS

MID-JUNE TO END OF SEPTEMBER

START: From Lake Louise Village follow the well-signed road uphill to Lake Louise and park in the large public parking lot. Head toward the Chateau, cross the bridge over the outlet creek and follow the lakeside path in front of the Chateau to the far end.

DIFFICULTY: Easy, well-maintained trail to start with, followed by moderately steep switchbacks and a final rocky scramble to the summit.

1. Fork right at a well-signed junction on the trail to Mirror Lake and Lake Agnes. The main trail heads around the lakeshore. Switchback up the broad, well-maintained path, ignoring any junctions to Mirror Lake. Turn right just before the lake.

2. Climb a few switchbacks to a junction where the trail to Little Beehive angles back to the right. Head toward Little Beehive, passing a trail that heads back left toward Lake Agnes. Watch for the St. Piran trail to the left in another 250 m.

3. Head up through delicate larch forest with ever-increasing views, then follow moderately steep switchbacks to the summit ridge. From here, scramble over loose, slabby rock to the broad, multi-cairned summit.

4. Either descend the way you came, with a detour to the teahouse, or traverse the mountain to the St. Piran/Niblock col and descend to the teahouse. See the option on page 48.

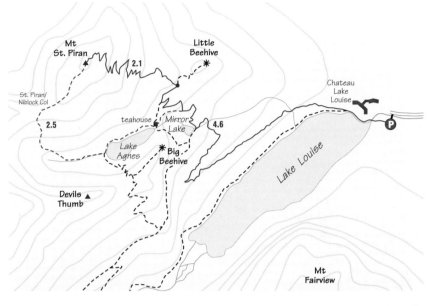

ABOVE: *The summit of Mount St. Piran. In the distance is Bath Glacier backdropped by Mount Daly.*

OPPOSITE: *Looking south toward Fairview Mountain on the left and mounts Haddo and Aberdeen, split by a glacier, on the right. The summit of Mount Temple is just visible in the background.*

Optional descent via St. Piran/Niblock col

You can traverse Mount St. Piran via the St. Piran/Niblock col, then descend to Lake Agnes. This route is more demanding, as it involves descending a steep boulderfield, then loose scree and dirt. It should not be attempted if the slope above the west end of Lake Agnes is snow covered.

1. Head southwest toward Mount Niblock and descend loose rock to the St. Piran/Niblock col.

2. Head down the steep, convex slope toward Lake Agnes. The trail initially trends right, then heads straight down to the rocky valley below, which is followed to the lake and teahouse.

TOP: *Mount Whyte (left) and Mount Niblock from the multi-cairned summit of Mount St. Piran.*

BOTTOM: *Mount Niblock with the St. Piran/ Niblock col out of sight to the right. On the descent from the col you need to trend right, toward the head of the valley, before descending to avoid the obvious cliffbands.*

12 Fairview Mountain

Delicate larches. Marmots and pikas and an incredible panorama of high, glaciated peaks.

DISTANCE: 10.4 km

HEIGHT GAIN: 1014 m

HIGH POINT: 2745 m

STRENUOUS

JULY TO END OF SEPTEMBER

START: From Lake Louise Village follow the well-signed road uphill to Lake Louise and park in the large public lot. Head toward the Chateau and look for a signed trail that heads into the forest near the viewpoint seats. If you park in the upper-level lot you'll see a trail from the west corner that joins the Fairview trail a short distance up from the trailhead (turn left).

DIFFICULTY: A good, though moderately steep, trail to Saddleback. The ascent of Fairview Mountain is steep rock and scree with snow patches early in the season.

1. Initially the trail passes a number of junctions, including one to the upper parking lot after about 100 m and one to the right to Fairview Lookout. Keep straight. Another junction a short distance beyond the Lookout junction leads to Paradise Valley and Moraine Lake. Bear right.

2. The trail now begins a sustained but moderate climb through forest and across avalanche slopes toward the Saddleback. At one point the trail briefly divides; stay left. The trail emerges into meadows and open larch forest and makes some final zigzags to the pass.

3. From the pass follow a trail to the right up an open slope toward the highest stands of larches. From here an obvious trail, with many variations, zigzags steeply up rock and scree to the summit.

Looking back toward Lake Louise from the open slopes of the Saddleback.

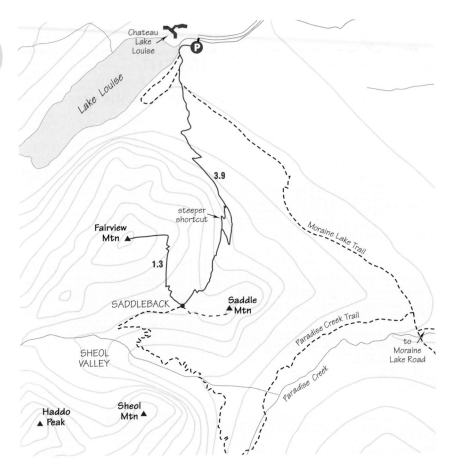

4. Descend the way you came. It is quicker and easier than any of the steeper "short-cut" routes back to the Saddleback.

Looking down onto Saddleback and Saddle Mountain from the route up Fairview Mountain, with the Sheol Valley beyond.

Caution: Do not, under any circumstances, attempt to descend directly to Lake Louise. The north ridge of Fairview Mountain is loose and very steep, with hidden cliff-bands. It has been the scene of fatalities and many rescues.

Note: It is possible to return to Lake Louise from Saddleback via Sheol Valley, Paradise Valley and Moraine Lake Trail. However, Sheol and Paradise valleys are subject to Group Access Regulations. Read "Group Access" on page 53 before considering this option.

TOP: *The route up Fairview from Saddle Mountain can be seen as a rising traverse from left to right. It is best to descend by your ascent route rather than by the steeper route to the right.*

BOTTOM: *Mount Victoria from the summit of Fairview Mountain.*

Easier option to Saddle Mountain

DISTANCE: 700 m from Saddleback

HEIGHT GAIN: 90 m above Saddleback

This little peak is often passed over in favour of the higher Fairview Mountain. It offers superb views down to Lake Annette and across to the massive bulk of Mount Temple. An option for hikers who don't want the steep, loose scramble up Fairview Mountain.

1. Scramble to the twin summits from the height of land.

2. Descend the way you came. Make sure you stay on the easy-angled ridge when you leave the summit, by avoiding false trails that lead onto steep ground to the left.

TOP: *Saddle Mountain from the Saddleback.*

BOTTOM: *The impressive north face of Mount Temple from the summit of Saddle Mountain. Lake Annette is the one bright spot in forested Paradise Valley.*

13 Larch Valley & Sentinel Pass

A premier Canadian Rockies experience. Feathery larches—gold in the fall—tranquil tarns, eroded pinnacles and outstanding views.

DISTANCE: 9 km return to Larch Valley, 11.6 km to Sentinel Pass

HEIGHT GAIN: 540 m, 725 m to pass

HIGH POINT: 2430 m

MODERATE

MID-JULY TO EARLY OCTOBER

START: Follow signs from Lake Louise Village uphill toward the lake. Turn left on Moraine Lake Road and drive 12 km to a large parking lot.

DIFFICULTY: A wide, well-maintained trail switchbacks moderately to the relatively flat valley. Moderately graded switchbacks lead up to Sentinel Pass.

Group access

The Moraine Lake area is often subject to access restrictions as a result of grizzly bear activity. Check at the visitor centre in Lake Louise before you head out.

Group access legally requires people entering the Moraine Lake backcountry to travel in a tight group of four or more. A tight group means that the person in the front must be able to comfortably speak with the person at the back at all times.

If you wish to hike when group access is in effect you should wait for other hikers at the trailhead and organize yourselves into a group. There is also a sign-up book outside the Lake Louise visitor centre.

1. Walk past the lodge to a trailhead sign and turn right. Climb through spruce and fir forest in a series of moderate switchbacks with improving views. At the top of the switchbacks you arrive at a junction with a welcome seat. Eiffel Lake is straight on. Bear right—no pun intended.

2. After a few minutes you enter Larch Valley and see the first stands of larches. The trail begins to swing right and climbs gently up a series of benches to the open upper valley. The imposing mass of Mount Temple is ahead to the right. To the left is Pinnacle Mountain. Arrive at a small tarn, one of the several Minnestimma lakes. This is the usual turnaround point for hikers who don't want to go on to Sentinel Pass.

However, the pass is worth visiting for the view of the pinnacles on the eroded ridge of Pinnacle Mountain and the panoramic view of the Ten Peaks.

3. From the lake the trail switchbacks up the steep slope to the pass. Head on up. It takes most people under half an hour. It is worth scrambling the short distance up to a viewpoint on the Mount Temple side of the pass.

4. Return the way you came. If group access is in effect, be sure to stay with a group all the way down.

A friendly chipmunk at Sentinel Pass. Chipmunks are smaller than golden-mantled ground squirrels (page 12) and have more stripes.

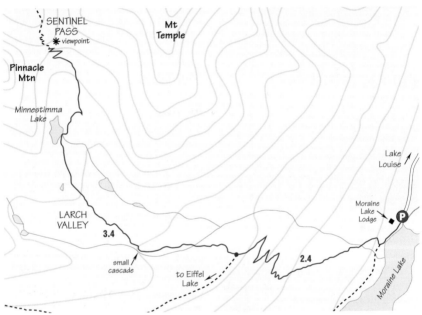

Note: At Sentinel pass you may be tempted to ascend Mount Temple. This is a scrambling route with serious route-finding difficulties due to the many off-route trails that have appeared in recent years. Don't go unless you have scrambling and route-finding experience on big mountains.

Note: It is possible to continue over Sentinel Pass and descend via Paradise Valley if you have left a second vehicle at the Paradise Creek trailhead. However, the initial descent is rough and Paradise Valley is a forest walk relieved only by Lake Annette. Group access, when in force, still applies. Not recommended.

Mount
?en

#7 Mount
Tuzo

#8 Deltaform
Mountain

#9 Neptuak
Mountain

TOP: *Nine of the Ten Peaks. Wenkchemna Peak, though a shoulder of Mount Hungabee, is regarded as #10.*

MIDDLE: *Snow-sprinkled mounts Allen (left) and Tuzo and Deltaform Mountain provide a background for the just-turning fall colours of Lyall's larches.*

BOTTOM: *The upper Minnestimma Lake with Sentinel Pass in the background. The southwest face of Mount Temple is to the right.*

OPPOSITE: *The Grand Sentinel on the north ridge of Pinnacle Mountain, from which Sentinel Pass gets its name.*

TOP: *The switchback trail to Sentinel Pass takes most people less than half an hour from the lake below.*

MIDDLE: *The broken ridge of Pinnacle Mountain with Mount Lefroy in the background, from the viewpoint just above the pass (3).*

BOTTOM: *Looking down on the pass with Larch Valley in the background.*

14 Eiffel Lake

Stunning views of the Ten Peaks across an impressive moraine-filled cirque with the option to climb to a high pass.

DISTANCE: 12.6 km return

HEIGHT GAIN: 365 m

HIGH POINT: 2255 m

MODERATE

JULY TO END OF SEPTEMBER

START: Follow signs from Lake Louise Village uphill toward the Lake. Turn left on Moraine Lake Road and drive 12 km to a large parking lot.

DIFFICULTY: A wide, well-maintained trail that switchbacks moderately to start with, then traverses easily under the slopes of Eiffel Peak.

Note: Read the section on group access on page 53 before heading out on this hike.

1. Walk past the lodge to a trailhead sign and turn right. Climb through spruce and fir forest in a series of moderate switchbacks. At the top of the switchbacks, 2.7 km from the parking lot, you arrive at a junction. Eiffel Lake is straight on.

2. The gradually ascending trail soon breaks out of the trees and traverses the lower, lightly treed open slopes of Eiffel Peak. Climb to a large boulder slope and pick your way across any lingering snow patches. Crest a slight rise and you will see Eiffel Lake below. The trail traverses a steep scree slope above the lake to a rocky promontory with larch trees and large rocks to sit on.

LEFT: *A hoary marmot.*

BOTTOM: *Mount Tuzo (left) and Deltaform and Neptuak mountains from the trail.*

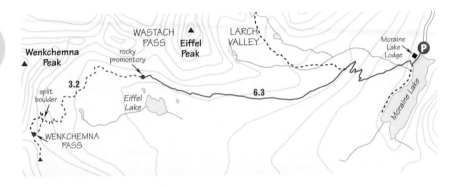

LEFT: *Approaching the rocky promontory (2), the usual turnaround point for those not wishing to continue to Wenkchemna Pass.*

BOTTOM: *Eiffel Lake with pale green larches in the foreground.*

The views of the Ten Peaks are stunning—they appear so close.

3. Return the way you came. If group access is in effect, be sure to stay with a group all the way down.

Going farther to Wenkchemna Pass

DISTANCE: add 6.4 km return

HEIGHT GAIN: add 330 m

HIGH POINT: 2611 m

Extend your hike later in the season when the snow has melted, to a high pass overlooking Prospectors Valley.

1. From the rocky promontory above Eiffel Lake the trail contours into the upper cirque of Wenkchemna Valley, switchbacking across rocky meadows to just below the pass. The old trail that swung right under the ridge of Wenkchemna Peak has been obliterated by the collapse of a rocky moraine, leaving a very unstable slope. A trail is now developing directly up moraine below the pass.

2. Turn left off the original trail at a large split boulder. After a short section of meadow, scramble up the moraine—a few cairns—to the pass.

TOP: *Heading up toward Wenkchemna Pass.*

BOTTOM: *The approach to Wenkchemna Pass. The route heads up a shallow valley to the right of the centre of the picture, then up the steep scree directly to the pass.*

3. It is worthwhile scrambling about 500 m up the ridge of Neptuak Mountain to a high point with cairn for an outstanding view of Opabin Pass and the head of Prospectors Valley.

TOP: *The white wooden notice on the pass has probably been chewed by a hungry porcupine.*

MIDDLE: *Looking toward Neptuak Mountain. It is worth scrambling to the cairn visible on the low ridge to the right.*

BOTTOM: *Mount Biddle with Opabin Pass, gateway to Lake O'Hara, to the right.*

15 Yoho Lake Loop

A forest-enclosed green lake with floral meadow and views of Takakkaw Falls across the Yoho Valley.

DISTANCE: 10.4 km loop

HEIGHT GAIN: 290 m

HIGH POINT: 1815 m

FAIRLY EASY

LATE JUNE TO END OF SEPTEMBER

START: Drive the Trans-Canada Hwy. to Yoho Valley Road, 3.6 km east of Field (the first junction to the right after the bottom of the hill if you are coming from Lake Louise). Drive Yoho Valley Road for 13.8 km to the parking lot at Takakkaw Falls. Although the trail starts from Whiskey Jack Hostel you can only park at the trailhead if you are staying at the hostel.

DIFFICULTY: A good, well-graded trail with moderately steep switchbacks at the start. The Iceline portion of the trail is rocky.

1. From the southern end of Takakkaw Falls parking lot, follow the paved tourist trail toward the falls. At the bridge, continue straight on to the trailhead near Whiskey Jack Hostel.

2. The trail switchbacks up avalanche paths to where a trail branches left to Hidden Lakes (an optional 600 m detour). Keep straight ahead and climb to a second junction to Yoho Lake. Keep left.

3. The trail makes a long, easy traverse across the hillside before climbing over a low ridge. The trail climbs easily through floral meadows and briefly alongside the creek while swinging around to the south end of Yoho Lake.

4. Continue around the lakeshore to the campground at a three-way junction. Left

heads 650 m to the forest-enclosed Yoho Pass. Keep right.

5. Follow Highline Trail, which climbs moderately steeply at first. The steepness relents and you begin a long, easy, undulating traverse through forest and across avalanche paths and scree slopes to merge with the Iceline trail. The view across the Yoho Valley is magnificent.

6. Turn right onto the Iceline trail (loose and rocky) and follow it down to the Yoho Lake junction (2). Keep left and return the way you came.

Takakkaw Falls, from Highline Trail, during a period of high runoff.

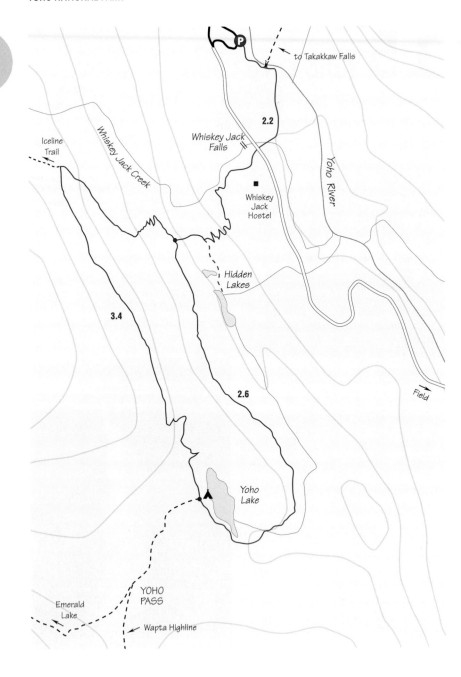

LEFT: *Yoho Lake and Wapta Mountain from near the backcountry campground.*

BOTTOM: *Daly Glacier above Takakkaw Falls and the Waputik Icefield from Highline Trail. The snow-covered peak to the left is Mount Balfour.*

63

16 Iceline–Celeste Lake Loop

A high, ascending traverse into a stark land of rocky moraines, sparkling glaciers, grey-green lakes, tumbling waterfalls and expansive views of snow-clad peaks.

DISTANCE: 19.1 km loop

HEIGHT GAIN: 730 m

HIGH POINT: 2230 m

STRENUOUS

MID-JULY TO END OF SEPTEMBER

START: Drive the Trans-Canada Hwy. to Yoho Valley Road, 3.7 km east of Field (the first junction to the right after the bottom of the hill if you are coming from Lake Louise).Drive Yoho Valley Road for 13 km to the parking lot at Takakkaw Falls. Although the trail starts from Whiskey Jack Hostel you may only park at the trailhead if you are staying at the hostel.

DIFFICULTY: A good, well-graded trail that climbs high above treeline. It is best avoided in poor weather, when you may wish to consider the less exposed hike #15 to Yoho Lake.

1. From the southern end of the Takakkaw Falls parking lot, follow the paved tourist trail toward the falls. At the bridge, continue straight on to the trailhead near Whiskey Jack Hostel.

2. The trail switchbacks steeply up a large avalanche path to where a trail branches left to Hidden Lake. Keep straight ahead and climb to a second junction to Yoho Lake. Turn right onto Iceline Trail.

3. Continue zigzagging upward across avalanche paths toward treeline and increasingly better views across the Yoho Valley. Arrive at a junction with Highline Trail, which heads back to Yoho Lake. Keep straight on.

4. The trail continues to climb steadily, zig-zagging to the top of a moraine where you get your first view of sparkling Emerald Glacier, now split into two parts. The trail now heads across the slope over talus and smooth limestone slabs with occasional cairns. Cross a creek just after a large, flat-topped rectangular rock and climb up and over the first of several lateral moraines. Meltwater from the glacier rushes down across slabs and boulders, forming a number of grey-green glacial lakes. This is the highlight of the trip. Arrive at the Celeste Lake connector junction.

5. The high point of the trail is atop the moraine about 800 m away and is worth a visit. Climb the small knoll for a better view.

6. Return to the Celeste Lake connector. You may decide to return the way you came so as to further enjoy the high alpine country. If you decide to complete the loop, turn left onto the connector.

7. The trail descends beneath moraine to a flowery alpine meadow and then into trees. Pass Celeste Lake (two lakes in low water conditions) and continue down to Little Yoho Valley. Just after Little Gem Pond, descend to the turbulent creek and cross the bridge. Turn right onto the Little Yoho Valley trail at the top of the bank.

8. Pass the junction to the Whaleback after a few metres. While it is possible for strong hikers to cross the Whaleback to Twin Falls, it makes for a long day (25.4 km and 380 m additional height gain. Continue descending to Laughing Falls and the junction

with the Yoho Valley trail, passing the junction with the Marpole connector (a strenuous hike across a rockpile) after 500 m.

9. Turn right and follow the Yoho Valley trail downhill to start with, then broad and almost flat, back to Takakkaw Falls.

TOP: *The remnants of Emerald Glacier below Michael Peak (4).*

BOTTOM LEFT: *Emerald Glacier.*

BOTTOM RIGHT: *Looking down from the first moraine to the creek crossing and the flat-topped boulder (4).*

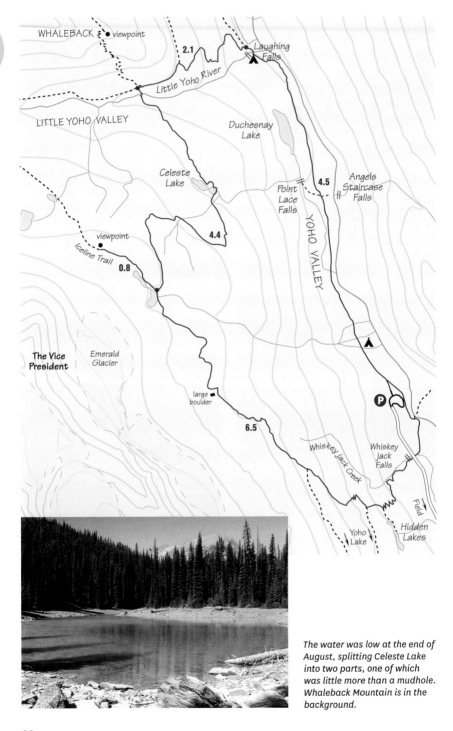

WHALEBACK ● viewpoint

2.1

Laughing Falls

Little Yoho River

LITTLE YOHO VALLEY

Duchesnay Lake

Celeste Lake

Point Lace Falls

4.5

Angels Staircase Falls

YOHO VALLEY

4.4

viewpoint

Iceline Trail

0.8

The Vice President

Emerald Glacier

large boulder

6.5

P

Whiskey Jack Creek

Whiskey jack Falls

Field

Yoho Lake

Hidden Lakes

The water was low at the end of August, splitting Celeste Lake into two parts, one of which was little more than a mudhole. Whaleback Mountain is in the background.

TOP: *The northern portion of Emerald Glacier under The Vice President from the Celeste Lake connector junction (4).*

MIDDLE: *Looking across barren talus toward the Little Yoho Valley from the small knoll above the high point of the trail (5). The glaciated peak is Mount McArthur, with Isolated Peak to the right.*

BOTTOM: *The meadows below Iceline Trail (7) are a refreshing contrast to the stark talus slopes above.*

17 Yoho Valley to Twin Falls

Spectacular waterfalls, raging torrents and a teahouse, with the option of alpine meadows and a high ridge with superlative views.

DISTANCE: 16 km return

HEIGHT GAIN: 300 m

HIGH POINT: 1820 m

MODERATELY STRENUOUS

JULY TO END OF SEPTEMBER

START: Drive the Trans-Canada Hwy. to Yoho Valley Road, 3.7 km east of Field (the first junction to the right after the bottom of the hill if you are coming from Lake Louise). Drive Yoho Valley Road for 13 km to the parking lot at Takakkaw Falls. Park in the northernmost parking area, just before the overnight parking only section.

DIFFICULTY: A wide, almost level trail to start, then a moderate, well-graded trail through trees for the rest of the way.

1. Walk through the overnight parking only area and continue on the trail and a short section of road to the campground and a trailhead kiosk.

2. Follow the wide, almost level trail up-valley across an open alluvial fan with a bridged creek. Pass a junction to viewpoints for Angels Staircase Falls (right) and Point Lace Falls a short distance to the left. Both are worth seeing.

3. The trail becomes narrower and climbs gently to a junction with a short trail to Duchesnay Lake. Continue to Laughing Falls and the junction with the Little Yoho Valley trail.

4. Continue up-valley for about 2 km through forest, crossing Twin Falls Creek to

Twin Falls Chalet.

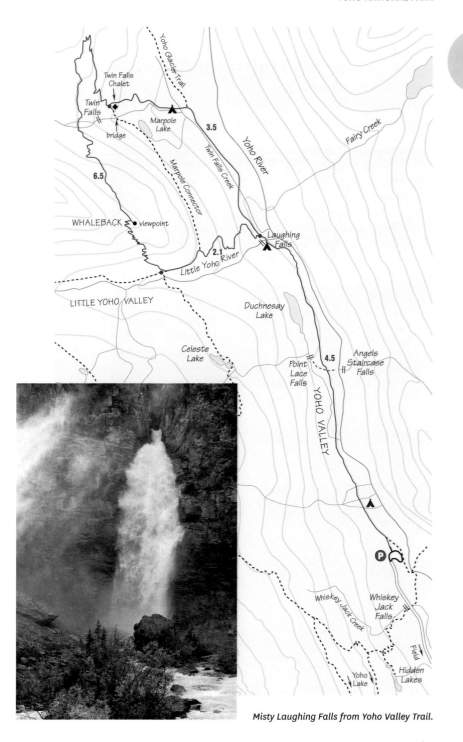

Misty Laughing Falls from Yoho Valley Trail.

TOP: *The lip of Twin Falls (2).*

BOTTOM: *Twin Falls.*

OPPOSITE: *Looking back down the trail toward Twin Falls Creek (3). The triangular snow-covered peak is Mont des Poilus.*

its east bank, and climb steadily to a junction with Yoho Glacier Trail.

5. Keep left on the main trail and climb moderately steeply with a few switchbacks. The roar of Twin Falls becomes louder and you arrive at a junction, and a map of the area. Turn left for Twin Falls Chalet. To the right is the trail to the Whaleback.

6. After viewing the falls, and maybe having afternoon tea, return the way you came.

Going farther to the Whaleback

DISTANCE: add 5.1 km

HEIGHT GAIN: add 285 m

A panoramic view of the Yoho Valley is the reward for taking this strenuous alternative return route. After the initial climb and descent to the very lip of Twin Falls, there is a delightful climb through subalpine meadows to the ridgetop.

1. From Twin Falls Chalet head back the way you came a short distance to the junction with the trail down to the Yoho Valley (5). Keep straight on.

2. A good dirt trail winds upward through forest to the foot of the cliffs, then climbs moderately beneath the rock walls until it is able to switchback steeply to the top. The trail then descends to emerge at the top of the cliffs near the falls. You can head across bare rock slabs to stand at the edge of the cascade. Take care! Scramble back to the trail and head for the bridge a short distance upstream. This is a seasonal bridge, so if hiking early in the season check at the information centre in Field to ensure it is in place.

3. The trail now ascends subalpine meadows in a series of easy switchbacks before traversing moderately steeply to the ridgetop. A cairn marks the descent trail to the right. Go straight for 85 m to the open ridgetop. Enjoy the panoramic view.

4. Retrace your steps to the cairn and turn left, immediately beginning a long series of switchbacks 300 vertical metres down a steep gully to Little Yoho Valley trail.

5. Turn left and follow the Little Yoho Valley trail down to Laughing Falls. Turn right on the Yoho Valley trail and reach Takakkaw Falls parking in 4.5 km.

18 Lake Oesa & Lake O'Hara

Lake O'Hara: the crown jewel of the Canadian Rockies. Blue lakes, green ponds, delicate larches, cascades and spectacular alpine views.

DISTANCE: 7.2 km return

HEIGHT GAIN: 240 m

HIGH POINT: 2285 m

MODERATE

MID-JULY TO END OF SEPTEMBER

START: Drive the Trans-Canada Hwy. 12.4 km west of Lake Louise and turn left onto the Lake O'Hara access road. Cross the railway tracks and immediately turn right on a gravel road which leads to the parking lots. Board the bus for Lake O'Hara if you have reservations (see page 6) or walk the access trail 11 km to the lake.

DIFFICULTY: Good, well-graded trail around the lake with some rocky sections on the trail to Lake Oesa.

1. Get off the bus at Le Relais day shelter. Head across the road toward the lake, past the warden cabin, and turn left on Lakeshore Trail. Follow it to the bridge over the outlet creek.

2. Cross the bridge and embark on the undulating trail along the north side of Lake O'Hara. Ignore the trail to Wiwaxy Gap that heads to the left after 400 m, and carry on to a junction where the Lake Oesa trail leaves Lakeshore Trail. Fork left.

3. The trail zigzags steeply to the top of a low rockband, then ascends more gradually up a series of rocky benches. Pass Yukness Lake. Ignore a junction to the right just before Victoria Lake and continue past Lefroy Lake to a high point on the trail and a four-way junction: Wiwaxy Gap and Abbot pass to the left, Yukness Ledge to the right.

4. Pick your way down to Lake Oesa on bits of trail and over slabs for a well-deserved break.

A bird's-eye view of Lake O'Hara from All Souls' Alpine Route. The low summits to the left are the Wiwaxy Peaks. In the background are Mount Huber and the long ridge of Mount Victoria.

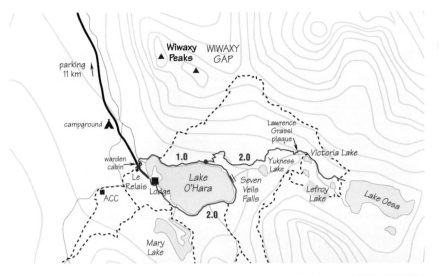

5. Head back the way you came to Lake O'Hara. At the junction by the lake turn sharply left on Lakeshore Trail, passing below Seven Veils Falls. Arrive at the junction with the rerouted East Opabin Trail (it is shown incorrectly on most maps).

6. Continue around the lakeshore, passing the West Opabin junction and arriving at a dock by Lake O'Hara Lodge. Turn left on a short trail that skirts the lodge and comes out on the road. Walk back along the road to Le Relais.

LEFT: *On the way to Lake Victoria. One of the many sets of steps built by Lawrence Grassi.*

RIGHT: *A plaque remembering Canadian Rockies trailbuilder Lawrence Grassi.*

TOP: *A little way after the Lawrence Grassi plaque there is a low waterfall featured in the watercolour "Below Lake Oesa" by Walter J. Phillips, a great Canadian painter and printmaker.*

MIDDLE: *Lefroy Lake.*

BOTTOM: *Lake Victoria and Ringrose Peak.*

TOP: *Large rock slabs by the shore of Lake Oesa make a good lunch spot.*

BOTTOM LEFT: *Mount Lefroy from the dock by Lake O'Hara Lodge (6).*

BOTTOM RIGHT: *Columbian ground squirrel by Lefroy Lake.*

19 Wiwaxy–Opabin Alpine Circuit

A steep ascent to a high col and a traverse of narrow, exposed rocky ledges provide a spectacular high-level tour of Lake O'Hara's two main alpine valleys.

DISTANCE: 10.1 km loop

HEIGHT GAIN: 600 m

HIGH POINT: 2532 m

STRENUOUS

MID-JULY TO END OF SEPTEMBER

START: Drive the Trans-Canada Hwy. 12.4 km west of Lake Louise and turn left onto the Lake O'Hara access road. Cross the railway tracks and immediately turn right on a gravel road which leads to the parking lots. Board the bus for Lake O'Hara if you have reservations (see page 6) or walk the access trail 11 km to the lake.

DIFFICULTY: A mixture of good, well-graded trails, narrow, exposed ledges and some minor scrambling. Don't attempt this route unless the Huber Ledges are completely clear of snow.

1. From Le Relais day shelter head toward the lake, past the warden cabin, and turn left on Lakeshore Trail. Follow it across the bridge over the outlet creek and continue for about 300 m to the Wiwaxy Gap trail.

2. Turn left and head up innumerable switchbacks through forest and across scree slopes with the occasional respite but increasingly better views. Finally a few turns across open scree bring you to Wiwaxy Gap.

3. Take a moment to view the next leg of your route, the Huber Ledges. It's easier than it looks. Head toward the mountain and shortly make a steep descent to the start of the ledges, which are followed in

a descending traverse with magnificent views across the face of Mount Huber to just above Lake Oesa. A steep descent brings you to the junction with the Lake Oesa trail about 200 m from the lake.

4. Pick your way down to Lake Oesa on bits of trail and over slabs for a well-deserved break.

5. Back at the junction head south on the Yukness Ledge trail. It initially angles toward the lake before dropping down to ford the outlet stream.

Watch for paint marks on the rocks indicating the best route. If the going becomes difficult or exposed you are off route.

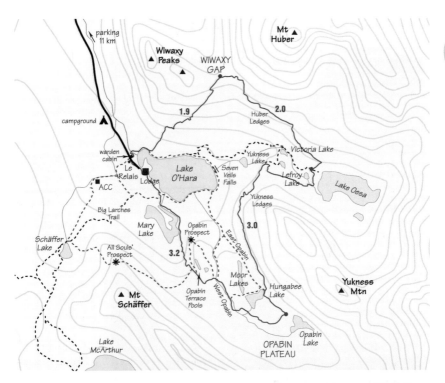

ABOVE: *The trail up to Wiwaxy Gap from Lake O'Hara.*

OPPOSITE: *Mount Biddle from a triple viewpoint a little way above Lake O'Hara on the trail to Wiwaxy Gap.*

TOP: *Crossing the Huber Ledges from Wiwaxy Gap in midsummer on a good trail.*

MIDDLE: *A narrow section of the Yukness Ledges trail.*

BOTTOM: *Rounding the corner toward Lake Oesa. At bottom right, the trail can be seen heading across slabby ground before turning rightward across the Yukness Ledges. From left to right are Mount Lefroy, Glacier Peak, Ringrose Peak and Yukness Mountain.*

Opabin Lake with Opabin Glacier and Pass to the right.

6. The trail climbs gradually over rocks and slabs before making a sudden descent to meet up with the shortcut trail from Victoria Lake. Turn left.

7. The route now follows a series of terraces and ledges, changing levels occasionally as it traverses across the lower slopes of Yukness Mountain toward Opabin Plateau. The ledges give way to a steep boulderfield which is first traversed and then descended to meet East Opabin Trail on the Opabin Plateau. Turn left for Opabin Lake.

There are many options here and two different routes back to Lake O'Hara (see dashed lines on map). I suggest and describe West Opabin Trail with a visit to Opabin Prospect, a superlative viewpoint. An alternative is to retrace your steps back to the Yukness Ledge junction and carry on down East Opabin Trail to Lake O'Hara Shoreline Trail, which can be followed either way around the lake to your starting point.

8. From Opabin Lake head southwest on West Opabin Trail, which switchbacks down to Hungabee Lake. Continue down, ignoring the cutoff to East Opabin Trail on

the right, to a junction just before a small pond (one of the Cascade Lakes). Turn left and cross the creek.

9. If you wish to visit Opabin Prospect—well worth the effort—turn right at the next junction and follow the trail through larches to the Prospect. After admiring the tremendous view over Lake O'Hara, continue on the trail past one of the Opabin Terrace pools to West Opabin Trail (a 750 m loop). Turn right.

10. After a few metres you will see the All Souls' Prospect trail heading off to the left. This is the route to take if you are hiking the option (page 81). Otherwise go straight on. You now begin a fairly steep zigzag descent to Mary Lake, traversing the slope below the sheer cliffs of Opabin Prospect. Follow the trail through trees around the north side of Mary Lake to a junction.

11. Turn right for the Lake O'Hara Shoreline Trail and Lake O'Hara Lodge or left for a more scenic route via the Alpine Meadow to Le Relais or the ACC hut. For Le Relais, keep right at all junctions except the last one 50 m above the road.

TOP LEFT: *One of the Cascade Lakes on an optional descent route just off the Opabin Prospect Trail.*

TOP RIGHT: *Wiwaxy Peaks from Opabin Prospect.*

BOTTOM: *Mary Lake with Lake O'Hara in the distance from West Opabin Trail.*

Extend the circuit via the All Souls' Alpine Route

DISTANCE: add 1.5 km

HEIGHT GAIN: add 285 m

HIGH POINT: 2475 m

This option is for the purist who wants to do the complete Alpine Route. It is a demanding uphill to a superb viewpoint followed by a steep, rocky descent to Schäffer Lake.

1. After descending from Opabin Plateau, pass both junctions to Opabin Prospect, and shortly after the second one, turn left on the All Souls' route (10). The rocky trail climbs moderately at first, then more steeply and at the end of the day seems more than 285 m. The reward is the marvellous view across Lake O'Hara to Wiwaxy Peak and Mount Huber.

2. It's all downhill from the Prospect—very steep, loose and rocky. Carry on across the ridge, following cairns, paint marks and sections of trail steeply downhill on the west side of the ridge to a junction with Big Larches Trail just before Schäffer Lake. Big Larches

ABOVE: *A cold September day on All Souls' Alpine Route. Amid the clouds are mounts Ringrose and Hungabee.*

BELOW: *All Souls' Prospect.*

Trail is rocky, rooty and involves extra height gain. Not recommended.

3. Turn left and arrive at beautiful Schäffer Lake in 100 m. Turn right at the junction by the lake to return to Lake O'Hara via the ACC hut. Carry on past the hut, keep left at a junction and cross the ridge to Le Relais.

20 Lake McArthur

A blue glacial lake with an impressive mountain backdrop, tranquil tarns and a larch forest.

DISTANCE: 7 km return

HEIGHT GAIN: 230 m

HIGH POINT: 2320 m

FAIRLY EASY

JULY TO END OF SEPTEMBER

START: Drive the Trans-Canada Hwy. 12.4 km west of Lake Louise and turn left onto the Lake O'Hara access road. Cross the railway tracks, turn immediately right on a gravel road and follow it to the parking lots. Board the bus for Lake O'Hara if you have reservations (see page 6) or walk the access trail 11 km to the lake.

DIFFICULTY: A good, well-graded trail with moderate height gain.

1. From Le Relais, follow the trail that leads away from the lake over a low ridge to alpine meadows. Continue past the ACC's Elizabeth Parker Hut and bear left up a forested draw. The trail zigzags up through forest to Schäffer Lake.

2. Cross the bridge over the outlet stream and carry on around the lake to a junction with McArthur Pass Trail.

3. Keep left on High-Level Trail, which at first follows the shoreline of Schäffer Lake, then climbs along the base of a rocky slope in open larch forest to a junction with Odaray Highline Trail. Keep straight on.

4. After 200 m there is another junction that marks the diversion of the Low-Level and High-Level trails. Keep straight on High-Level. Continue climbing toward a cliffband which is easily negotiated with some scrambling.

5. The trail moderates above the cliffband and climbs to a ridge with a cairn overlooking Lake McArthur. Descend easily to the lake, ignoring various side trails. At the lake, a side trail to the left leads to a rocky vantage point.

6. Follow the trail around the lake (another side trail leads to the outlet stream) and turn to your right into a shallow draw

Schäffer Lake with Mount Huber and Wiwaxy Peaks hazy from forest-fire smoke.

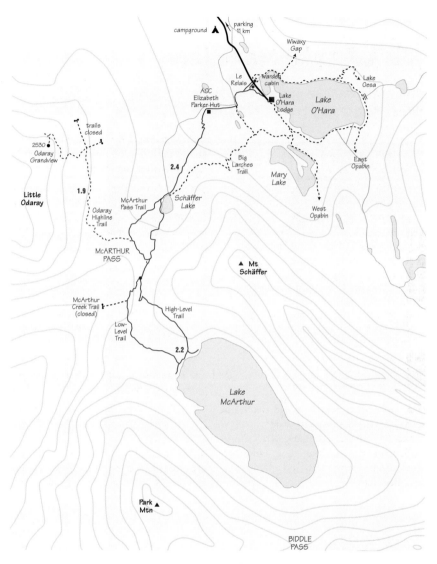

leading down the valley. Crest a slight rise and follow the trail past a small tarn (McArthur Pool) to the treed valley and the junction with McArthur Creek Trail.

7. Keep right and soon reach your ascent trail. Turn left. The Odaray Highline junction is reached in 200 m. Turn left, then right at the next junction onto McArthur Pass Trail, which leads back to Schäffer Lake.

8. Turn left at Schäffer Lake and retrace your ascending route back to Lake O'Hara.

Big Larches Trail is an alternative way back from Schäffer Lake, but it is rocky, rooty, involves extra height gain and is not recommended.

TOP: *Approaching the easy scramble up the cliffband (4).*

BOTTOM: *Lake McArthur with Mount Biddle in the haze. The yellow flowers in the foreground are cinquefoil.*

OPPOSITE TOP: *Lake McArthur with Mount Biddle (left) and Park Mountain viewed from the rocky trail up to Odaray Grandview. A little farther down the trail you get a view of the Goodsirs.*

OPPOSITE BOTTOM: *Remnants of glacier on Mount Odaray seen from Odaray Grandview.*

Extend your hike to Odaray Grandview

DISTANCE: add 3.8 km
HEIGHT GAIN: add 310 m
HIGH POINT: 2530 m

Odaray Grandview offers a "grand view" of Lake O'Hara and the surrounding mountains. Experienced hikers will find it worthwhile, though a bit of a grunt.

Note: In the past this trail has been subject to limited access, with only three parties a day allowed. At the time of writing this has been discontinued, but may be reimplemented if the bear situation warrants.

1. On your return from Lake McArthur, instead of turning right onto McArthur Pass Trail (6) keep straight on Odaray Highline. The trail climbs gently through flower meadows and then contours across the lower slopes of Little Odaray to a four-way junction. Two of the trails are closed, so your only option is to turn left onto the alpine route to Odaray Grandview.

2. The trail, marked with blue and yellow rectangles, climbs moderately at first into a small, rock-strewn bowl, then more steeply up and around cliffbands and along rocky ledges, finally emerging on the edge of a plateau at a small cairn. There are two alternatives here: up and to the right gives a close up view of the small glacier on Mount Odaray, while to the left and up brings you to the large Grandview cairn. Enjoy the view—you've earned it.

3. Return the way you came, turning left onto McArthur Pass Trail to take you back to Schäffer Lake.

21 Emerald Lake Circuit

A superb short, scenic nature walk around an "Emerald" lake with varied views and changing vegetation.

DISTANCE: 5.4 km loop

HEIGHT GAIN: negligible

HIGH POINT: 1300 m

EASY

JUNE TO END OF SEPTEMBER

START: Drive the Trans-Canada Hwy. to Field. Head west from Field for 1.6 km to Emerald Lake Road and follow it for 9 km to its end. The trailhead is at the far end of the parking lot.

DIFFICULTY: Easy, well-maintained trail. Can be enjoyed in either direction. Here it is described clockwise.

1. Don't cross the bridge to the lodge. From the trailhead, head clockwise around the lake on the trail, paved to start with, crossing a large avalanche path to a scenic viewpoint. Seats along the lakeshore allow you to rest and enjoy the view of shapely Mount Burgess back across the lake and Wapta Mountain (home to the Burgess Shale World Heritage Site) to the east.

2. A few sections of old horse trail still exist. When in doubt choose the trail closest to the lake. Arrive at the junction with the Emerald Basin trail (see option).

3. Keep right and follow the north shore across a large alluvial fan created by the outwash from the President Range. Ignore a trail to Yoho Pass to the left. Continue to the inlet bridge, which is crossed to the east shore.

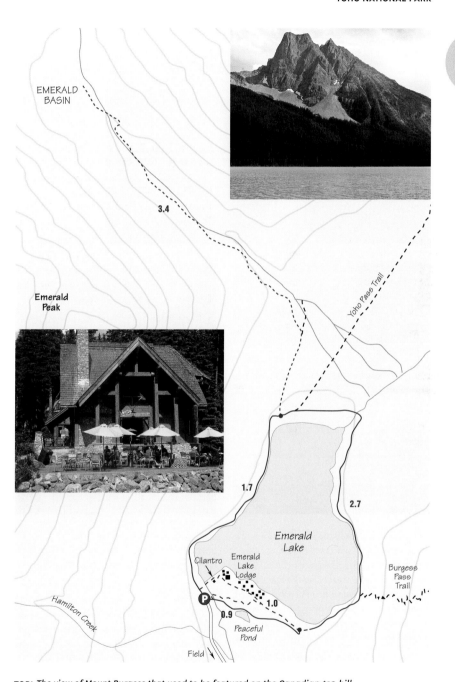

EMERALD
BASIN

3.4

Emerald
Peak

Yoho Pass Trail

1.7

2.7

Emerald
Lake

Cilantro

Emerald
Lake
Lodge

Burgess
Pass
Trail

P

1.0

0.9

Hamilton Creek

Peaceful
Pond

Field

TOP: *The view of Mount Burgess that used to be featured on the Canadian $10 bill.*

BOTTOM: *Cilantro Bar and Restaurant.*

OPPOSITE: *Emerald Lake Lodge from the interpretive viewpoint near the start of the trail.*

TOP: *The trail across the flats at the head of the lake. Wapta Mountain in the background.*

BOTTOM: *Hiking Emerald Lake is certainly not a wilderness experience. There are many activities other than hiking to entertain you and lots of photographic opportunities.*

4. The trail now leads into dense, moist forest, a surprising contrast to the west and north shores. This illustrates the effect of the microclimate created by the lake and its surrounding mountains. Follow the cool, damp trail to the beginning of the south shore where it turns right and arrives at the Burgess Pass junction. Keep straight on.

5. After about 500 m you reach a junction where the trail to Peaceful Pond branches off to the left. It provides the shortest way back to the parking lot and avoids the lodge complex. You can, if you wish, continue straight on, skirting behind the lodge and across the bridge to your starting point.

Immediately on the lodge side of the bridge is Cilantro, a bar and restaurant open from 11:00 a.m. to 9:00 p.m. mid-June to mid-September. There is a concession window where you can purchase soft drinks and snacks.

Going farther to Emerald Basin

DISTANCE: add 6.6 km to hike around lake
HEIGHT GAIN: 225 m
HIGH POINT: 1540 m

This moderately steep trail leads to an enclosed, avalanche-swept basin beneath The President and The Vice President.

1. From the junction at the north end of Emerald Lake (2) the trail heads up a lightly treed gravel slope to a junction. Turn left. The trail to the right is an old horse trail which soon becomes washed out.

2. Climb moderately to start with, up a rocky trail through the forest. The trail then descends slightly through trees and emerges into the open valley. Cross a large avalanche path to meet the creek.

3. Cross a small side creek (dry later in the season) and follow a good trail to the left that heads toward the twin waterfalls. The trail crosses open talus slopes before petering out among the rocks below the falls.

4. Return the way you came.

TOP: *Twin waterfalls drain the high cirque below Mount Carnarvon.*

BOTTOM: *The entrance to Emerald Basin. This high cirque is ringed by Emerald Peak, Mount Carnarvon, Mount Marpole (seen above), The President and Vice President and Michael Peak.*

22 Emerald Triangle

Western red cedar forest, spectacular views down to Emerald Lake and across to the President Range. Mountain goats.

DISTANCE: 20.3 km loop

HEIGHT GAIN: 880 m

HIGH POINT: 2180 m

VERY STRENUOUS

MID-JULY TO MID-SEPTEMBER

START: Drive the Trans-Canada Hwy. to Field. Head west from Field for 1.6 km to Emerald Lake Road and follow it for 9 km to its end. Park at the near end of the parking lot and look for an unsigned trail that leads down some steps to the right (east).

DIFFICULTY: Moderately steep; rocky on Yoho Pass Trail. This is a strenuous outing for fit hikers. The legs of the triangle are Burgess Pass Trail, Wapta Highline Trail and Yoho Pass Trail.

1. Head down the steps and across a bridge. Keep on the main trail at a junction shortly after the bridge and hike past Peaceful Pond to meet Shoreline Trail. Turn right and continue for about 500 m to Burgess Pass Trail, where the lakeshore trail turns left along the east shore.

2. Turn right and immediately begin the relentless climb through thick forest of spruce, pine and western red cedar. The only consolation: it's cool on a hot day, the grade is moderate and you are getting the worst of the climb over with. You finally emerge on an open ridge with views of Mount Burgess and down to Emerald Lake.

3. Continue climbing to where the trail forks. To the right is the junction with the trail from Field. Keep climbing here to an excellent viewpoint, then descend to rejoin the official trail a few metres below. To avoid the climb you can head right to the junction, turn left and contour around on the main trail.

4. Turn left (east) on Wapta Highline Trail, which descends slightly to the lowest point of the pass in trees, finally breaking out into the open on the slopes of Wapta Mountain. Here it turns north and contours across rocky alpine slopes, passing two junctions to the Burgess Shales (see note opposite).

The trail finally emerges from thick forest, the steep north face of Mount Burgess in profile (2).

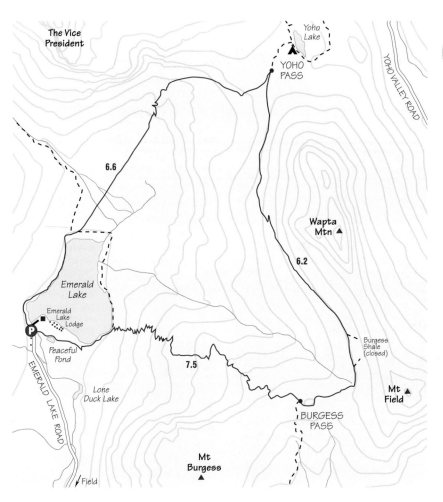

Note: On the Wapta Highline section of this trail you will pass signs advising you that the World Heritage Burgess Shale beds are closed to the public. Don't be tempted to sneak in—the fines are high. If you wish to visit you will need to take a tour guided by Burgess Shale Geoscience Foundation staff: 1-800-343-3006, burgess-shale.bc.ca/hikes.php.

5. Just after crossing a rockslide below Wapta Mountain the trail descends in a couple of switchbacks, then traverses across five avalanche paths, the last one below a rock wall, before dropping into the forest to the junction at Yoho Pass.

Picturesque Yoho Lake is only 650 m along the trail to the right and worth a visit if you have not been there before. See trail #15.

6. From the junction, head west toward Emerald Lake. The rough, rocky trail descends steeply across open slopes and rockfall to the head of the alluvial fan at the head of Emerald Lake. Hike down the gravel trail through sparse trees for almost 2 km to a junction just before the lake.

7. Turn right and follow the west shore of the lake back to the parking lot, ignoring all trails to the right.

Heading north across the open slopes of Mount Field toward Wapta Mountain (4). The Burgess Shales are up to the right.

A Burgess Shale Geoscience Foundation guided group at the rockslide (5). The President Group is in the background.

Creeping beardtongue, often called purple penstemon, grows profusely amid the shale by the side of the trail.

TOP: *Looking down to Emerald Lake from the rockslide (5).*

BOTTOM LEFT: *The trails around here are not always bare and dry. Crossing the alluvial fan toward the lake (6).*

BOTTOM RIGHT: *Descending from Yoho Pass below waterfalls cascading down the steep wall of Michael Peak.*

23 Bow Glacier Falls

A 120-m waterfall in a rocky glacial basin, with the option of experiencing the Wapta Icefield's high-mountain realm of rock and ice.

DISTANCE: 9.6 km

HEIGHT GAIN: 135 m

HIGH POINT: 2080 m

FAIRLY EASY

JULY TO END OF SEPTEMBER

START: Drive the Icefield Parkway north from the Trans-Canada Hwy. for 36 km to Num-ti-jah Lodge. The trailhead parking area is on the left side of the access road by public washrooms before you reach the lodge.

DIFFICULTY: Well-trodden trail, flat for most of the way. Occasionally under water, but there is an alternative, higher trail available. The final section is across talus.

1. Ignore the trail by the trailhead kiosk and continue down the road past the lodge and a signed trailhead on the left side of the parking area.

2. Cross the inlet stream and follow the trail along the north shore to the gravel flats at the southwest corner of the lake. Depending on water level, you can either hike across the flats (cairns) or follow a gently undulating trail on higher ground to the right. Arrive at the beginning of a canyon.

3. The trail now climbs steeply up some steps to the rim of the canyon and a junction below which a large limestone boulder bridges the gorge. The trail to Bow Hut (see option) crosses this boulder. Keep right and continue climbing to the crest of a terminal moraine and a good view of the falls.

4. Descend into the basin and hike across talus to the base of the falls.

5. Return the way you came.

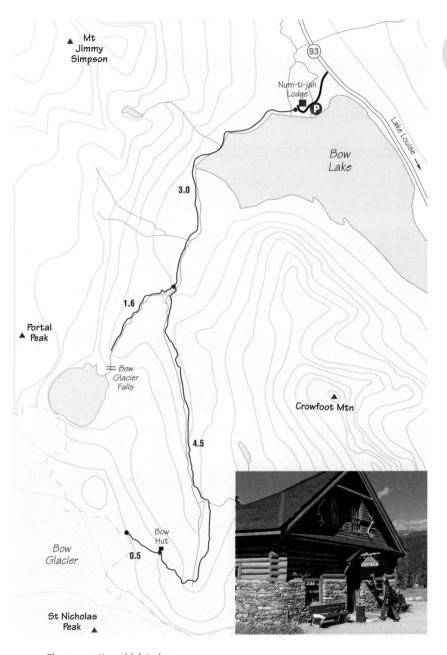

93

Mt Jimmy Simpson ▲

Num-ti-jah Lodge

P

Bow Lake

Lake Louise →

3.0

1.6

Portal Peak ▲

Bow Glacier Falls

Crowfoot Mtn ▲

4.5

Bow Glacier

Bow Hut

0.5

St Nicholas Peak ▲

ABOVE: *The store at Num-ti-jah Lodge.*

OPPOSITE: *Looking across Bow Lake to the gravel flats leading up toward the falls. Sharp-pointed St. Nicholas Peak is to the right.*

TOP: *Heading along the shoreline of Bow Lake. That umbrella could only be protection from the sun on this virtually cloudless day.*

MIDDLE: *A group of hikers gets close up to the thundering cascade of the lower part of the falls.*

BOTTOM: *Because of its north-facing aspect and the surrounding high cliffs, Bow Glacier Falls gets little sunlight.*

Going farther to Bow Hut

DISTANCE: 15.4 km return to hut
HEIGHT GAIN: 475 m
HIGH POINT: 2420 m

More of an alternative than an option. The Alpine Club of Canada's Bow Hut, one of the largest of the high mountain huts, is located just below a spur of the Wapta Icefield beneath St. Nicholas Peak. If you wish to stay at Bow Hut, contact The Alpine Club of Canada at 403-678-3200, www.alpineclubof-canada.ca.

1. Cross the chockstone (3) where the trail to Bow Glacier Falls branches right. There is one high step-up on a small foothold initially, then a few feet of scrambling onto the broad top.

2. Follow a well-trodden path to the right that leads up through trees, then drops down to the creek. Continue upstream, ascending a steep rockslide at the resumption of the canyon, to the canyon edge. The trail continues through trees and across talus near the edge of the canyon. At the end of the canyon climb steeply into a high cirque with steep cliffs at its head. You can see the hut at the top of the cliffs opposite.

3. Near the head of the cirque the trail goes to the right, crosses several streams and heads for the right-hand side of a gap in the cliffs. Follow cairns marking a discernible trail across this section. Zigzag up steep moraine to a shallow upper valley. Bow Hut is located near the upper right-hand edge of the valley, at the top of steep cliffs.

4. Follow a trail up talus above the hut for about 500 m for a view of the small glacier under St. Nicholas Peak that allows mountaineering access to the Wapta Icefield above. This is a popular area for winter ski mountaineering.

5. Return the way you came.

TOP: *Scrambling over the chockstone (O1).*

BOTTOM: *The canyon leading up to the cirque below Mount Olive.*

TOP AND LEFT: *Bow Hut, and its interior kept in immaculate condition while occupied by a climbing school.*

BOTTOM: *St. Nicholas Peak and the bare ice (mid-August) of the small glacier leading up to the Wapta Icefield.*

24 Helen Lake

Easy access to flowery meadows with alpine lakes, stunning views, hoary marmots and an easy peak for the more energetic.

DISTANCE: 13.8 km to ridge above lake

HEIGHT GAIN: 570 m

HIGH POINT: 2520 m

MODERATELY STRENUOUS

JULY TO END OF SEPTEMBER

START: From the Icefields Parkway at 33 km north of the Trans-Canada Hwy. at Lake Louise and 7.7 km south of Bow Summit. Trailhead parking is on the east side of the road, opposite the Crowfoot Glacier viewpoint.

DIFFICULTY: A well-graded trail, moderately steep in places. The ascent of Cirque Peak is a non-technical scramble up scree with one easily negotiated rock band.

1. The trail ascends at a moderate grade through light subalpine forest, then steepens as it ascends the side of an open slope and rounds the end of the ridge into more open terrain.

2. The grade eases and the trail works its way into the open subalpine cirque below Cirque Peak. Rock-hop across Helen Creek and ascend gently to Helen Lake.

3. Don't stop too long by the lake. Head for the ridge above the lake, where the panoramic view is well worth the extra 125 m of height gain. Most people turn around here. If you want to extend your day, see the two options on the following pages.

4. Return the way you came.

TOP: *The trail above Helen Creek soon after breaking out of the trees. The haze is from forest fires in British Columbia.*

BOTTOM: *Cirque Peak from Helen Lake.*

ABOVE: *Helen Lake from the ridge leading over to Dolomite Pass.*

LEFT: *Looking down onto the wide expanse of Dolomite Pass, Katherine Lake to the right. The other small lakes are unnamed.*

Going farther to Dolomite Pass

DISTANCE: add 5.2 km

HEIGHT GAIN: extra 125 m to the pass on return

An excursion to Katherine Lake and the barren alpine region of Dolomite Pass.

1. From the top of the ridge above Helen Lake, descend 125 m to Katherine Lake and follow the faint trail to a small lake in the environs of Dolomite Pass.

2. Return the way you came. Back up to the ridge!

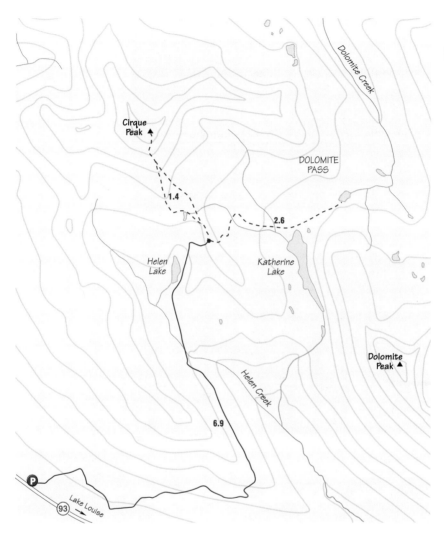

Scramble up Cirque peak

DISTANCE: add 2.8 km to east summit
HEIGHT GAIN: 473 m from ridge
HIGH POINT: 2993 m

An easy, non-technical ascent to a fabulous viewpoint.

1. The route can be seen from the ridge above Helen Lake. Head across rock and scree to pick up the trail that ascends the open scree slope to the ridge or scramble onto the end of the ridge.

2. Follow the ridge to the west summit. An easy scramble will take you to the marginally higher east summit, where you can sign the summit register.

3. Descend the way you came.

TOP: *The route up Cirque Peak can be clearly seen in this picture.*

MIDDLE: *View to the south from the summit.*

BOTTOM: *Bow Lake and the Wapta Icefield from the summit of Cirque Peak.*

25 Chephren & Cirque Lakes

Quiet lakes below imposing peaks and steep cliffs. Worth hiking if you are staying in the campground.

DISTANCES FROM TRAILHEAD RETURN: Chephren Lake 7 km; Cirque Lake 8.4 km; both lakes 12.8 km

HEIGHT GAIN: 250 m (75 to Chephren)

HIGH POINT: 1795 m

FAIRLY EASY

MID-JUNE TO END OF SEPTEMBER

START: Waterfall Lakes campground, on the Icefields Parkway at 58 km north of Lake Louise and 19 km south of Saskatchewan River Crossing. If you are not camping there ignore the campground entrance and continue along the service road to a parking area on the left.

DIFFICULTY: While there is little height gain, both trails can be wet in places. The trail to less-visited Cirque Lake is a little longer, steeper and rougher walking.

1. From the end of the parking area head straight downhill on a good track (chain across it) to the trailhead by the Mistaya River bridge at the west end of the campground. The bridge is behind campsite 87.

2. Cross the bridge and ascend gradually through forest to a junction. Chephren Lake right, Cirque Lake left. The Chephren Lake trail is the shorter and flatter of the two alternatives.

3. Turn right and follow the rooty trail through moderately thick forest, with a large, long meadow to your left for most of the way to Chephren Lake. You are immediately below the steep east face of Mount Chephren. Howse Peak is to the left.

4. Return to the Chephren–Cirque junction and keep straight on (or turn left if heading back to the campground). Head gently downhill, make a sharp right turn, then climb to meet the outlet creek. The trail,

ABOVE: *A common loon on Chephren Lake. It is depicted on the Canadian $1 coin—the Loonie.*

RIGHT: *Chephren Lake and Mount Chephren.*

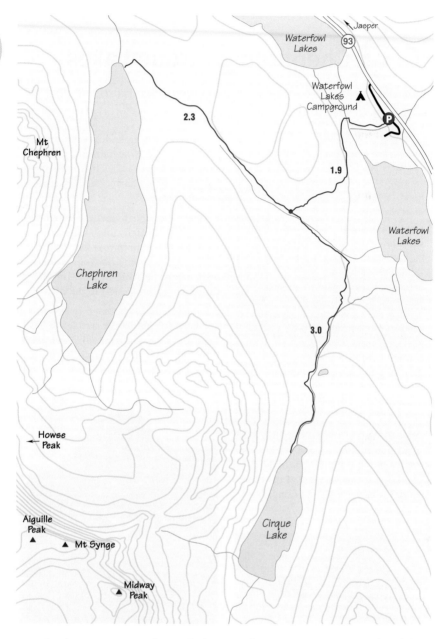

steep in places, stays near the creek the rest of the way to the lake. At a couple of places the trail divides. Go either way. The trail ends at a large boulder field with resident marmots. The mountains that make up this impressive cirque are, from left to right, Stairway, Aries and Midway peaks. The little summit to the left is unnamed.

5. Return the way you came.

TOP: *Cirque Lake below the steep cliffs of Midway Peak. The hoary marmots that inhabit the boulderfield seem unafraid of human visitors.*

BOTTOM LEFT: *Cirque Lake outlet creek (4).*

BOTTOM RIGHT: *White bog orchids.*

26 Nigel Pass

Easy hiking up an open valley with scattered forest, avalanche slopes and flower-filled meadows. Views into the remote Brazeau backcountry.

DISTANCE: 14.4 km return

HEIGHT GAIN: 370 m

HIGH POINT: 2210 m

MODERATE

MID-JULY TO MID-SEPTEMBER

START: Trailhead parking is along a dirt road on the east side of the Icefields Parkway, 8.5 km south of the Banff–Jasper Park boundary and 900 m north of the Bridal Veil Falls lookout, at the top of the big bend hill.

DIFFICULTY: An easy-angled, well-graded trail until the final kilometre, where it climbs 160 m moderately steeply to the pass over into the Brazeau.

1. Head down the gated access road a short distance before turning right and descending to a bridge over Nigel Creek.

2. Cross the bridge to the east side of Nigel Creek and follow the trail through light forest and across several avalanche slopes to Camp Parker, a historic and prehistoric site in a large group of Engelmann spruce.

3. Ignore various side trails and continue up-valley on the same side of the creek. The valley becomes more open and you pass through a succession of meadows. Arrive at a junction with a horse trail to the left.

4. Keep straight on the main trail and shortly began a moderately steep climb to

The open valley beyond Camp Parker. The orange-coloured ridge is the head of the valley. The trail crosses a pass just left of the centre of the picture. The true Nigel Pass is to the left.

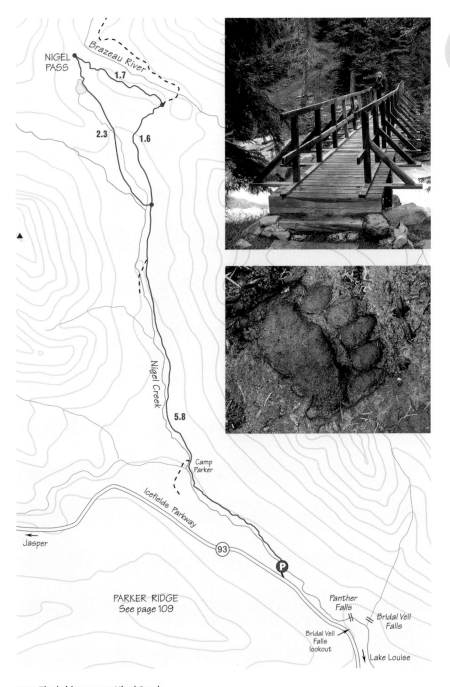

TOP: *The bridge across Nigel Creek.*

BOTTOM: *A reminder that this is grizzly country.*

the pass where a post marks the boundary between Banff and Jasper national parks.

5. Rather than continuing down the trail into the Brazeau drainage, I suggest you head left along the rocky ridge for ever improving views into the Brazeau back-country. After 1.7 km, drop down to the true Nigel Pass (it's the farthest of the two possible passes), where you will find a rarely used horse trail.

6. Head south on the trail past a small lake, cross back into Banff National Park and continue down to the outlet creek from the lake. Cross the creek and follow the trail down-valley to the main creek. Head left on the true left side of the main creek, recross the small creek and scramble up the bank to rejoin your ascent trail.

7. Return the way you came.

TOP: *Hiking the rocky ridge above the Brazeau River.*

BOTTOM: *The small lake on your return route from Nigel Pass.*

27 Parker Ridge

A good, short trail to stretch your legs when driving the Icefields Parkway. Spectacular bird's-eye view into the vastness of the Columbia Icefield.

DISTANCE: 6.6 km return

HEIGHT GAIN: 280 m

HIGH POINT: 2280 m

FAIRLY EASY

MID-JULY TO MID-SEPTEMBER

START: Parker Ridge is halfway along the Icefields Parkway between Lake Louise and Jasper. The trailhead is on the west side of the road, 4.2 km south of the Banff–Jasper Park boundary and 5.2 km north of the Bridal Veil Falls lookout, at the top of the big bend hill.

DIFFICULTY: A fairly easy, well-maintained trail that switchbacks up to a ridge overlooking the Saskatchewan Glacier valley. The trail was upgraded in 2016 with new signage and waymarking cairns.

Note: Because of heavy use and delicate alpine terrain, Parks Canada closes this trail until it is dry enough for hiking. If you wish to hike it before mid-July, check with the information centre in Banff or Jasper to make sure the trail is open.

1. From the parking area head upward through light forest of Engelmann spruce and subalpine fir, switchbacking to treeline in about a kilometre. Cross a large talus slope and continue switchbacking to the crest of the ridge.

2. The official trail veers left and descends from the saddle before petering out on the side of the ridge with good views of Castleguard Mountain and the rapidly receding Saskatchewan Glacier.

Hikers descending the lower section of the trail. The peak in the background is an unnamed point on a ridge of Mount Athabasca.

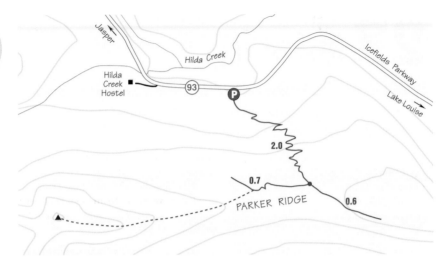

3. Return to the saddle and climb to a broad knoll with a couple of rock wind shelters and good views to the north and northwest. If you need exercise, it is possible to continue up the ridge to a smaller knoll.

4. Return the way you came.

TOP: *Saskatchewan Glacier leading up to the Columbia Icefield, with Castleguard Mountain in the distance.*

BOTTOM: *The small knoll behind the figures can be climbed for more expansive views.*

28 Wilcox Pass & Wilcox Peak Ridge

High alpine meadows, bighorn sheep, snow-covered Mount Athabasca and a panoramic view of some of the highest glaciated peaks in the Canadian Rockies.

DISTANCE: 10.8 km return
HEIGHT GAIN: 560 m
HIGH POINT: 2600 m
MODERATELY STRENUOUS
MID-JULY TO MID-SEPTEMBER

START: Drive 108 km south of Jasper on Icefields Parkway (3.2 km south of the Icefield Centre) or 123 km north of Lake Louise. Turn east into the Wilcox Creek campground entrance road and park on the left after a few metres. For hikers staying at the Columbia Icefield campground there is a steep unofficial trail leading to the ridge (1) from walk-in site #7.

DIFFICULTY: Good trail, steep in a few places early on. Snow-covered most of June and usually wet until the end of July.

Approaching Wilcox Pass. Mount Wilcox in the background.

1. From the parking lot follow the steep trail through mature Engelmann spruce and subalpine fir, breaking out of the trees for good after 1.5 km onto an open ridge with superb views of Mount Athabasca and the Athabasca Glacier.

2. Continuing uphill the trail climbs moderately steeply by Wilcox Creek before reaching the alpine tundra of the pass. A large pile of rocks with a sign marks the official summit. The actual summit is about 800–900 m farther.

3. Look for a narrow trail, just beyond the official summit, heading left toward the ridge. Climb over a bump and up to the edge of the broad ridge (about 1.1 km and 240 m height gain). Revel in the panoramic view of Mount Athabasca and the Columbia Icefield.

4. Return the way you came.

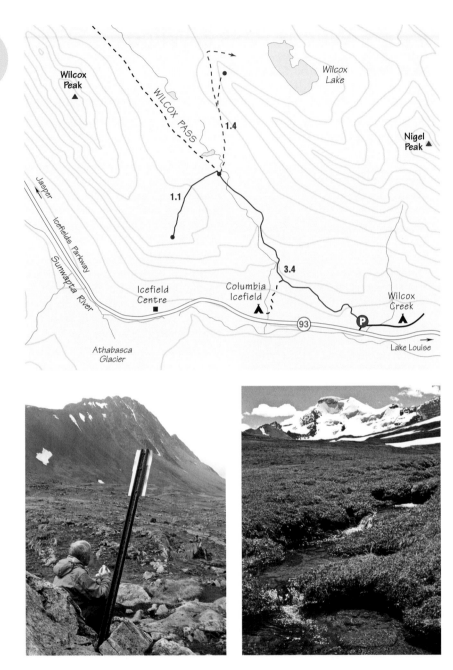

LEFT: *The official summit of the pass is marked with a cairn on top of a pile of rocks.*

RIGHT: *The north face of Mount Athabasca from the meadows of Wilcox Pass.*

TOP LEFT: *Rocky Mountain bighorn sheep are often seen on the slopes around Wilcox Pass.*

TOP RIGHT: *The gleaming north face of Mount Athabasca from Wilcox Peak Ridge.*

MIDDLE: *A rainy day near the summit of Wilcox Pass.*

BOTTOM: *The toe of Athabasca Glacier from Wilcox Peak Ridge in 1974. Compare it with what you see today to see how fast the glacier is receding.*

Going farther to Wilcox Lake

DISTANCE: 1 km from pass

HEIGHT GAIN: 120 m

HIGH POINT: 2515 m

This option will take you to a viewpoint for an isolated lake beneath the west face of Nigel Peak. It is possible to traverse into this remote cirque to explore the environs of the lake.

1. From the marker at the top of the pass head northeast toward the northwest ridge of Nigel Peak, staying on higher ground to avoid the bog. Contour up and across the slopes of the northwest ridge of Nigel Peak and look for a good trail heading up and across steep talus to the ridge. From here the sloping basin with Wilcox Lake at its head is laid out before you.

If you would like to explore the basin, head farther to the northwest to a lower col, reached by a steep rock and scree slope. As you cannot see the lake from here, you may wish to climb a little way up the ridge to a cairn. It is easy to traverse into the cirque from here.

2. Return the way you came.

Wilcox Lake is situated in a remote and fascinating high alpine valley with slabby rocks, little pools, high alpine plants, colourful lichen (middle) and interesting features such as patterned ground (bottom).

29 Geraldine Lakes

Picas and marmots abound in the boulderfields of this long valley with tranquil lakes, rushing cascades and high alpine cirques.

DISTANCE: 10.5 km to second lake

HEIGHT GAIN: 405 m to second lake

HIGH POINT: 1890 m

MODERATELY STRENUOUS

JULY TO MID-SEPTEMBER

START: From Jasper, drive south on the Icefields Parkway (Hwy. 93) for 30 km to Hwy. 93A junction at Athabasca Falls. Follow Hwy. 93A for 1.2 km to Geraldine Lake Fire Road, then 5.4 km to the end of the narrow, bumpy road.

DIFFICULTY: Easy to first lake, then steep hills, rough, muddy, rooty, loose rocks and boulders—slippery when wet. This trail is for strong hikers. Take your time and consider turning back from Second Geraldine Lake if conditions are bad.

1. From the trailhead kiosk the trail heads up moderately steeply, followed by an easy downhill to First Geraldine Lake.

2. The usually muddy path heads around the west shore to a waterfall at the end of the lake and the end of the good trail.

3. Follow an obvious path through rocks and scramble steeply up the right side of the waterfall for about 90 vertical metres, emerging onto a rocky bench.

4. Angle left to the southeast side of the valley—small cairns may mark the way. Relocate the path, which soon disappears at another talus field. Look for yellow markers. Cross the creek, skirt the edge of a small pond on rocks and relocate the trail in the trees. The trail leaves the trees and

First Geraldine Lake. The mountain is a subsidiary peak on the north ridge of Mount Fryatt.

crosses open, rocky terrain, coming close to a second waterfall.

5. The trail then climbs very steeply up a gully to the left of the waterfall on dirt and loose rocks for about 100 vertical metres to the top of the headwall.

6. Continue less steeply up a talus slope to the crest of a ridge overlooking Second Geraldine Lake. Descend easily about 60 m to the lake by some trees. For many this will be the end of the trail.

7. If you are heading for the campground at the end of Second Geraldine Lake, follow the trail around the east shore, rock-hopping across several boulderfields. The campground is across the creek (bridge near outlet), 6.1 km from the trailhead.

8. Return the way you came.

TOP LEFT: *The waterfall by the trail (3).*

TOP RIGHT: *The second waterfall, above the rocky bench (4).*

BOTTOM: *Shortly after you reach the top of the headwall above First Geraldine Lake, you arrive at a rocky area with intermittent ponds. Head to your left (to the right in this picture) and pick the easiest line close to the ponds. The trail becomes obvious again at the far end of the larger pond.*

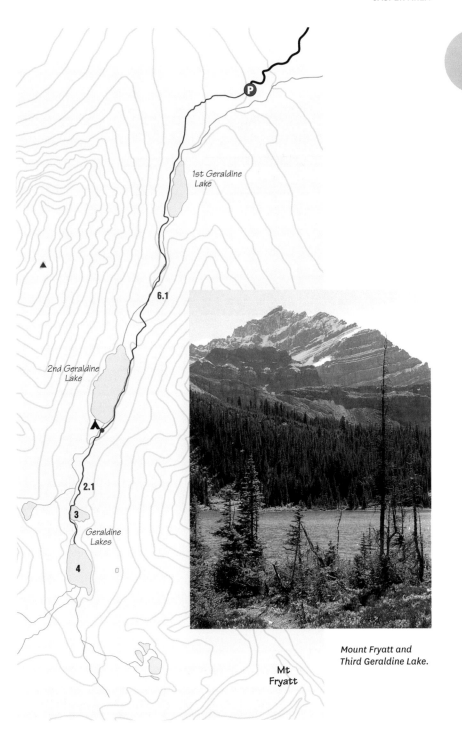

1st Geraldine
Lake

6.1

2nd Geraldine
Lake

2.1

3

Geraldine
Lakes

4

Mt
Fryatt

*Mount Fryatt and
Third Geraldine Lake.*

Going farther to Third and Fourth Geraldine lakes.

DISTANCE: 2.1 km to Fourth Lake

HEIGHT GAIN: 80 m to Fourth Lake

HIGH POINT: 1980 m

Strong hikers will want to continue to Fourth Geraldine Lake. It is a bit of a struggle getting to Third Lake through bush and across boulderfields, but once there you are in more open country near the head of the valley.

1. Continue on the east side of the creek across from the campground and follow a good but rough trail marked by cairns in places to Third Geraldine Lake.

2. Cross the creek just below the outlet to the west shore of Third Lake and follow a trail along the shore and through meadows to Fourth Geraldine Lake.

3. Return the way you came.

TOP: *Second Geraldine Lake, the largest of the four and the usual turnaround point.*

BOTTOM: *You finally break out into the alpine at Fourth Geraldine Lake. There is a high alpine cirque with several small lakes under the west face of Mount Fryatt that would be well worth exploring,*

30 Cavell Meadows

Flowery alpine meadows from mid-July to mid-August, the towering north face of Mount Edith Cavell, and Angel Glacier.

DISTANCE: 8.3 km for all trails

HEIGHT GAIN: 370 m

HIGH POINT: 2288 m

MODERATE

NO DOGS

ROAD OPEN MID-JUNE TO MID-OCTOBER, BUT SEE NOTE BELOW

START: From Jasper drive south on the Icefields Parkway (Hwy. 93) for 6.7 km to Hwy. 93A junction. Follow Hwy. 93A for 5.2 km to Mount Edith Cavell Road. The narrow, winding road (drop-off area for trailers at the start) ends after 13.8 km at Edith Cavell parking lot.

DIFFICULTY: A very popular, well-graded, moderately steep trail. Arrive early to beat the crowds and get the best lighting on Angel Glacier.

Note: Because of heavy use and delicate alpine terrain, Parks Canada closes this trail until it is dry enough for hiking. If you wish to hike it before mid-July, check with the information centre in Jasper to make sure the trail is open.

1. From either exit from the parking lot, follow Path of the Glacier Trail to a junction where it continues straight on.

2. Turn left onto Cavell Meadows Trail, which switchbacks over and along the foot of a lateral moraine. Continue steeply through subalpine forest to a junction at 2.1 km. This is the start of the circuit trail.

3. Keep straight on. The trail soon arrives at the meadows with good views of Mount Edith Cavell and Angel Glacier. At the southern end of the meadows there is a fork in the trail.

4. Turn right onto a 100 m spur trail to a viewpoint.

5. Return to the main trail and continue on it for 240 m to another junction. Keep right. The trail to the left is a shortcut offering an abbreviated circuit.

6. Continue to another junction. The trail to the right climbs to a superb viewpoint on a ridge above the meadows (500 m distance and 100 m height gain).

7. Return to the main trail, which descends to the junction at the start of the circuit (2).

8. Descend your upcoming route to the junction with Path of the Glacier Trail (1). Turn left uphill, then descend to Cavell Pond with its miniature glacier and icebergs. Follow Path of the Glacier Trail back to the parking lot.

This hoary marmot seems to enjoy the attention of the crowd from among the boulders at the foot of the lateral moraine (2).

TOP: *Angel Glacier on the north face of Mount Edith Cavell from the trail at (7).*

MIDDLE: *Hiking up by the lateral moraine (2). The marmot on the previous page was photographed here.*

BOTTOM: *Heading up toward the high point (6). Unfortunately the cloud was rolling in.*

TOP: *Flower-filled meadows on the lower portion of the descent trail (7).*

Purple saxifrage (MIDDLE) *and moss campion* (BOTTOM) *are found at higher elevations on this trail.*

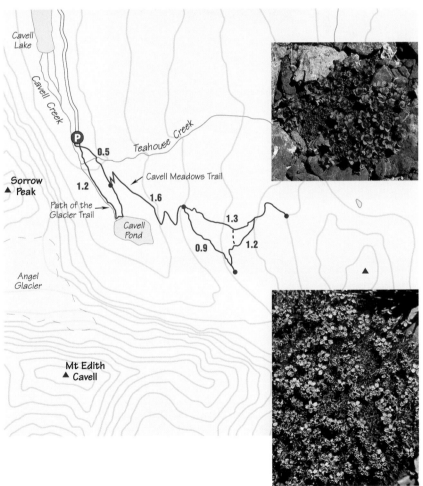

TOP: *Descending the side of the moraine toward Cavell Pond. Note the small remnant glacier that breaks apart to produce the icebergs.*

MIDDLE AND BOTTOM: *Icebergs in Cavell Pond on Path of the Glacier Trail (8).*

31 Valley of the Five Lakes

Clear, blue-green lakes of varied hue in a forest setting. A popular family outing as well as a good destination during inclement weather.

DISTANCE: 6.4 km

HEIGHT GAIN: 105 m

HIGH POINT: 1135 m

EASY

MID-MAY TO END OF OCTOBER

START: From Jasper, drive south on the Icefields Parkway (Hwy. 93) for 8.8 km to a parking lot, enlarged in 2016, on the east side shortly after the bridge over the Athabasca River.

DIFFICULTY: A very popular, well-graded trail system that was improved for the centennial in 2017. Some sections of trail are heavily used by cyclists.

1. From the parking lot follow the trail through lodgepole pine and across the boardwalk protecting the Wabasso Creek wetlands. Arrive at a four-way junction (trail #9). Left leads, in about 8 km, to Old Fort Point near Jasper, while right goes to Wabasso Lake in about 5.5 km.

2. Keep straight on trail #9a. Climb to a junction, the start of the loop around the lakes. You can hike the circuit either way. I prefer clockwise for the best views.

3. Keep left. Cross a ridge and descend to the southeast end of First Lake. Bear right and arrive at a junction. The trail to the left leads to the far end of First Lake and continues through forest to Old Fort Point. Turn right.

4. The trail (#9a) now crosses open hillside above Second, Third and Fourth lakes to a junction between Fourth and Fifth lakes. If you turn right you can shorten the circuit

by 1.8 km. The point of land between Third and Fourth lakes makes a good lunch spot.

TOP: *The boardwalk across Wabasso Creek (1).*

BOTTOM: *Beavers have been busy alongside the trail working at felling this 15″ diameter tree.*

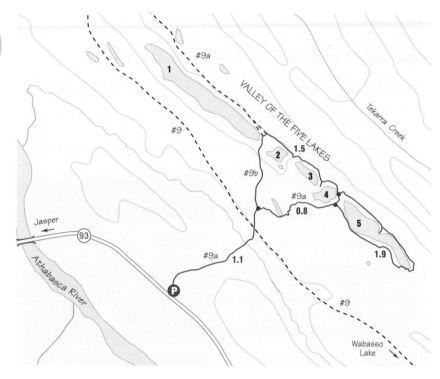

First Lake, looking northwest.

5. Keep left and make a circuit of Fifth Lake on a narrower trail. Arrive back at a junction between Fourth and Fifth lakes just above the bridge over the creek.

6. Turn left, bearing left when in doubt, to reach the junction at the beginning of the circuit (2).

7. Keep left and follow trail #9a back to the parking lot.

TOP: *Dry conditions in recent years have reduced Second and Third lakes to small ponds. This photograph was taken in mid-June (2007) when you would expect water levels to be high.*

MIDDLE: *Fourth Lake taken in the early nineties when water levels in the area were much higher.*

BOTTOM: *Looking down Fifth Lake. The boats in the foreground can be rented for fishing from Online Sport & Tackle or Currie's Guiding, in Jasper.*

32 Mina Lake–Riley Lake Circuit

Scenic lakes that can be easily reached from Jasper by those without their own transportation. Birdwatchers and photographers will enjoy Cottonwood Slough.

DISTANCE: 9 km return

HEIGHT GAIN: 230 m

HIGH POINT: 1290 m

FAIRLY EASY

YEAR-ROUND

START: From the information centre in Jasper, head north on Elm St. (immediately to the west) to Pyramid Lake Road. Turn right. The trailhead is at the back of a large parking lot opposite the Aquatic Centre.

DIFFICULTY: Well-maintained trail, moderately steep at first. These trails are part of Jasper's numbered routes system. You will be following trails #8 and #2.

BELOW: *Mina Lake.*

OPPOSITE: *The small slough on the way to Mina.*

1. The trail is a few metres up the bank above the back of the parking lot. Head left behind townhouses and uphill through forest. At a junction stay right. Cross Cabin Lake Service Road and continue on trail #8, ignoring any junctions. Pass a small slough and arrive at Mina Lake.

2. Continue along the shore of Mina Lake to a junction. Cabin Lake is 800 m to the left if you wish to extend your hike and visit it.

3. Turn right and follow trail #8, keeping left at a junction with #8c, which leads back through forest to the Cabin Lake service road. Arrive at Riley Lake.

4. Continue around the end of Riley Lake, turning right on trail #8 at the next junction. Descend through forest and follow the trail alongside Cottonwood Slough, the best birdwatching and beaver habitat

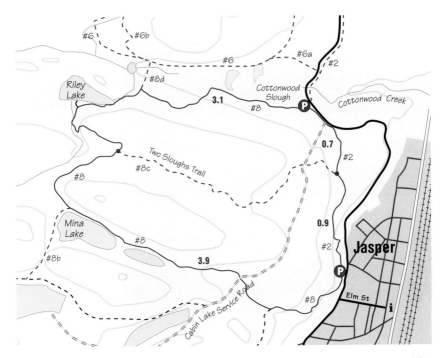

around Jasper, back to a small parking lot off Pyramid Lake Road.

5. Turn right onto trail #2. Cross Cabin Lake Service Road and, at the junction with #8c, go straight. After a short uphill, begin a long descent to the parking lot opposite the Aquatic Centre.

Options

While I have described one of the more popular circuits in the area, you can see from the map above that there are many options. All the trails are well signed.

• At the end of Mina Lake you can turn left and visit Cabin Lake. You should probably return the same way, as the wide swath of the Cabin Lake service road does not make for good hiking.

• You can extend your walk to take in Patricia Lake by following #8d to Patricia Lake Circle Trail (#6) instead of turning right on #8. When you reach #6 you have the choice of

turning right along the north side of Cottonwood Slough or heading left to Patricia Lake. Return using #2 or head south on #6 to #6a.

• Trails farther north between Patricia and Pyramid lakes see heavy horse traffic.

TOP: *Riley Lake.*

MIDDLE: *Cabin Lake Service Road runs through the wide firebreak protecting the town of Jasper.*

BOTTOM: *Cottonwood Slough, with Pyramid Mountain in the background.*

33 Opal Hills

The Opal Hills were named by Mary Schäffer in 1908 for the opal-like colours of the abundant wildflowers she found there. Shorter but steeper than the Bald Hills trail.

DISTANCE: 8.2 km

HEIGHT GAIN: 470 m

HIGH POINT: 2160 m

FAIRLY EASY

NO DOGS

MID-JULY TO MID-SEPTEMBER

START: From Jasper east entrance, drive east on Hwy. 16 for 1.8 km to Maligne Lake Road. Turn right and cross the bridge over the Athabasca River. Shortly after, bear left at a junction and drive about 44 km to Maligne Lake. Turn left into the main parking lot and bus drop-off just before the lodge. Keep left and drive to the highest parking lot. The trailhead is straight ahead as you enter the lot.

DIFFICULTY: A relentlessly steep trail to start, then a gentle walk down an alpine valley behind two small hills.

A wary mule deer a short way up the trail.

1. From the parking area the trail descends slightly to cross a boggy meadow. Pass a junction with Lakeshore Trail and arrive at a junction with Mary Schäffer Loop. Fork left.

2. The trail enters a dense forest of lodgepole pines and climbs relentlessly to a junction—the start of the actual loop.

You have a choice here. The right-hand trail is very steep but gets you above treeline sooner. The left-hand trail is less steep and the valley walk affords better views.

3. I prefer to head left through forest and flowery subalpine glades to treeline, where the trail heads to the right and enters a valley behind two low hills.

4. Hike gently downhill toward a creek coming in from the left. As you approach the creek you will notice that there appear to be three different trails ahead. You want to end up on the highest one.

5. Just after crossing the creek, head slightly left and up to the highest trail.

6. The trail to the left leads back to the creek, where there is a fork (the left-hand trail is a scramblers trail to Opal Peak, while the trail to the right soon peters out in flower meadows by some small cascades). Turn right and arrive at a signed four-way junction in 200 m.

7. The trail straight ahead is overgrown and not recommended. To get a view down to Maligne Lake and across to mounts Unwin and Charlton, turn left and climb steeply up the ridge for about 400 m and follow a short trail to the right to a good viewpoint.

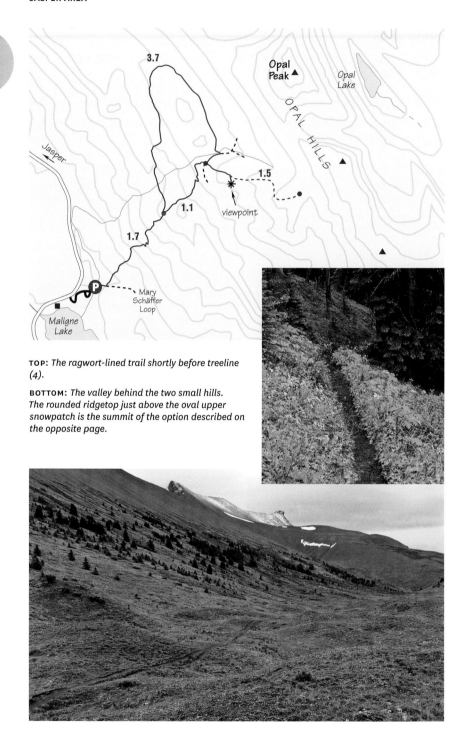

3.7

Opal
Peak ▲

Opal
Lake

OPAL HILLS ▲

Jasper

1.5

1.1

viewpoint

1.7

▲

P

Mary
Schäffer
Loop

Maligne
Lake

TOP: *The ragwort-lined trail shortly before treeline (4).*

BOTTOM: *The valley behind the two small hills. The rounded ridgetop just above the oval upper snowpatch is the summit of the option described on the opposite page.*

See the option for the continuation of the trail up the ridge.

8. Back at the four-way junction continue straight ahead and follow the main trail very steeply down to the junction that ends the loop. Turn left and descend to the parking lot.

Option Opal Ridge

DISTANCE: add 3 km return

HEIGHT GAIN: add 300 m

This option extends your hike to a small grassy summit with good views.

1. From the four-way junction follow the trail up the ridge with ever-improving views of Maligne Lake and across to the Bald Hills. The ridge ends on a small knoll.

2. Head right, picking your way over small scree and trending rightward to the ridge overlooking Maligne Lake. Follow this around to the left up easy scree to a small grassy summit—an outlier of the higher un-named peak above.

3. Return the way you came.

TOP: *Looking down on the two small hills from flower meadows by the creek (6).*

BOTTOM: *The north end of Maligne Lake from the ridge leading to the grassy summit (O2).*

34 Bald Hills

Superb views of Maligne Lake. Open subalpine wildflower meadows allow you to wander to higher viewpoints.

DISTANCE: 12.5 km

HEIGHT GAIN: 640 m

HIGH POINT: 2330 m

MODERATELY STRENUOUS

NO DOGS

MID-JULY TO MID-SEPTEMBER

START: From Jasper east entrance, drive east on Hwy. 16 for 1.8 km to Maligne Lake Road. Turn right and cross the bridge over the Athabasca River. Shortly after, bear left at a junction and drive about 44 km to Maligne Lake. Follow the road to its end at a parking lot. The trailhead is the old gated fire road to your right as you enter the parking lot.

DIFFICULTY: The broad dirt road climbs easily and steadily all the way with an option at one point of a steeper shortcut.

1. The trail climbs steadily through an open forest of lodgepole pine. Ignore all side trails and keep your eyes open for a signed junction with a narrow trail to the left at 2.5 km.

2. You have two alternatives here. The trail to the left is steeper and shorter, the one to the right easier but longer. I suggest you head right, leaving the steeper trail for the descent.

3. Continue on the fire road passing a junction with the Evelyn Creek Loop trail on your right. Arrive at the site of an old fire lookout (horse trail) with limited views of Maligne Lake. Look for the signed upper junction of the shortcut trail 90 m beyond the lookout site—your descent route.

Maligne Lake from the rounded summit (4). The high mountain is Samson Peak, with snow-covered Malign Mountain to its right.

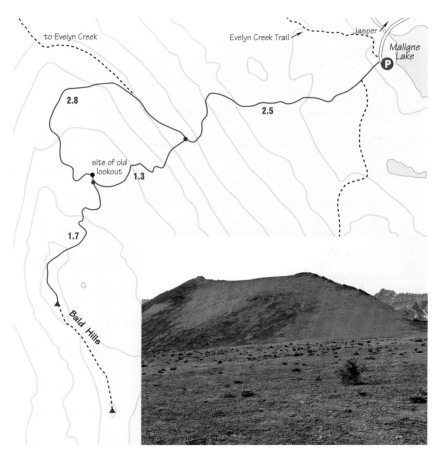

TOP: *The small, rocky peak (5) from the rounded summit (4). It's an easy walk to the top, and well worth it.*

BOTTOM: *Mount Charlton (left) and Mount Unwin from the rocky peak (5). In the distance are the Mount Brazeau group beyond the south end of Maligne Lake.*

4. After a breather, follow the trail southward to the foot of a small, rounded summit, then zigzag steeply to the top.

5. The small, rocky peak to the south with a cairn on top is a worthy objective. There is a good trail to the top.

6. Retrace your steps to the previously noted junction and follow the shortcut trail down to the fire road.

TOP: *Looking south along the ridge from the summit of the small, rocky peak (5). It is possible to extend your hike along the ridge and explore the high alpine country beyond.*

BOTTOM: *Nearing the bottom of the shortcut trail (6). The trail, originally a horse trail, is a little rooty in places but saves you 1.5 km.*

35 Little Shovel Pass

A shaded forest walk to a high pass set in open flower meadows and alpine tundra, with the option of a scenic ridgewalk.

DISTANCE: 21 km return

HEIGHT GAIN: 550 m

HIGH POINT: 2240 m

STRENUOUS

NO DOGS

JULY TO END OF SEPTEMBER

START: From Jasper east entrance, drive east on Hwy. 16 for 1.8 km to the Maligne Lake Road. Turn right and cross the bridge over the Athabasca River. Shortly after bear left at a junction and drive about 44 km to Maligne Lake. Follow the road to its end at a parking lot. There are two trailheads on your right as you turn in to the parking lot. The one you want is to the right. The other gated dirt road leads up to The Bald Hills.

DIFFICULTY: The trail is well graded and climbs gently for the first 5 km. It then switchbacks more steeply, breaking out of the trees a little way beyond Little Shovel campground. This is a long day out, so start early.

1. From the trailhead the trail follows a gentle grade all the way to the Evelyn Creek campground. On the way it passes a junction to Lorraine Lake, which is 140 m away to the left, and a little farther on, a junction to Mona Lake 200 m to the right. Neither lake is particularly interesting.

2. From Evelyn Creek campground the trail, still in the trees, begins to switchback more steeply, reaching Little Shovel campground at just under 8 km.

3. Continuing upward, the trail breaks out of the trees, affording outstanding views as you approach the pass.

4. Once at the pass consider ascending the small, unnamed peak to the northeast. See option.

5. Return the way you came.

Approaching Little Shovel Pass.

Option: A scenic ridgewalk

DISTANCE: add 1.1 km
HEIGHT GAIN: add 240 m
HIGH POINT: 2480 m

The ridge to the northeast of Little Shovel Pass provides a scenic ridgewalk with views of the open tundra hereabouts that provides grazing for a small caribou herd.

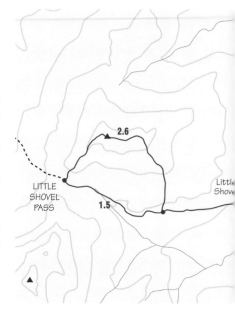

1. From the pass ascend grass and scree slopes to the northeast, working your way up onto a small, rocky peak at the end of a short ridge.

2. At the far end of the ridge, drop down to a rounded knoll, then head directly south following open ground down toward the main trail. On the opposite side of the valley are two prominent creeks. Lower down you should be descending an open ridge that points directly between the two creeks.

3. When you get to the trees, contour to the right, keeping to the open as much as possible until you arrive at the main trail.

BELOW: *The rocky peak at the end of the ridge (O1). The finger rock on the cairn points to Big Shovel Pass, on the route of the Skyline Trail.*

OPPOSITE TOP: *Looking into the head of Snow Bowl from the rocky peak. The top of Mount Hardisty can be seen above the long ridge of the Maligne Range. Few people stop to explore these high alpine cirques.*

OPPOSITE BOTTOM: *The descent route from the southeast end of the ridge follows the open slopes down to the forested valley.*

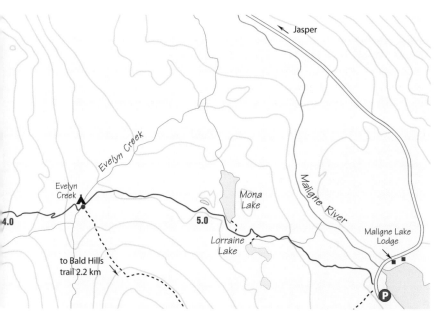

36 Sulphur Skyline

Stunning views of the serrated limestone ranges of eastern Jasper National Park. Your reward: a soak in the Miette Hot Springs pool.

DISTANCE: 9.4 km return

HEIGHT GAIN: 640 m

HIGH POINT: 2050 m

MODERATE

MIETTE HOTSPRINGS ROAD IS OPEN FROM MID-MAY TO EARLY OCTOBER

START: From Jasper, follow Hwy. 16 east for about 40 km to Miette Hotsprings Road at Pocahontas. If you are coming from the Edmonton direction, the junction is 7 km from Jasper Park's east gate. Turn south and drive 17 km to the Miette Hotsprings. Park at the far end of the parking lot. The trailhead is to the right of the pool complex at the head of the drop-off loop.

DIFFICULTY: A steady, steep, dry ascent on a well-graded trail with a steep final scramble up a stony path to the summit. There are lots of seats on the way.

Caution: Do not attempt to descend the northwest ridge to the hot springs. You will encounter steep, loose, dangerous terrain and miserable forest with cliffbands.

1. Follow the wide, paved path steadily uphill. The paving ends and the trail narrows, climbing relentlessly to a junction. Left is Fiddle River and Mystery Lake. Keep straight on.

2. The trail continues steeply with many leg-aching switchbacks compensated for by views opening up across flower-filled meadows. Finally the trail levels off on a broad shoulder below the summit. Note the large white boulder.

3. It's an easy walk across a small meadow to the final scramble to the summit where you are rewarded with a stunning view. To the southeast is the gravelly valley of the Fiddle River. South and west is the Miette Range and to the northwest the steeply tilted limestone of Ashlar Ridge.

4. Return the way you came.

TOP LEFT: *Expansive views open up to the southeast.*

TOP RIGHT: *Bighorn sheep on the ridge leading to the summit.*

BOTTOM: *James's saxifrage in the rocks near the top.*

OPPOSITE: *The trail heads up onto the summit cone from the shoulder. The large boulder of white quartzite is a glacial erratic that was deposited here during the ice ages.*

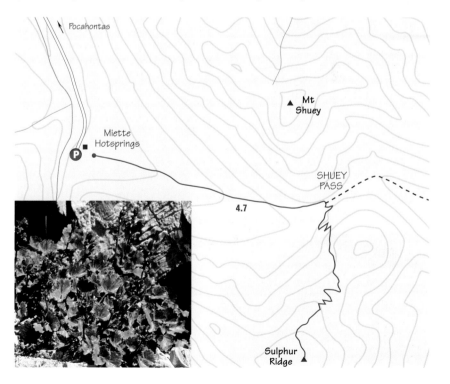

TOP: *Looking down from the summit into the Fiddle River valley.*

BOTTOM: *From the summit you can see a tempting ridge below with a trail along it. I don't recommend this as a way to descend. See the caution on page 138. If you do decide to hike the ridge you should return by the same route. It may be possible to traverse below the summit on a sheep trail to your ascent trail. I haven't done it.*

37 Virl, Dorothy & Christine Lakes

These low-elevation, forest-enclosed lakes are less crowded than trails closer to Jasper and offer early- and late-season hiking or respite from the sun on a very hot day.

DISTANCE: 10.1 km return

HEIGHT GAIN: 275 m

HIGH POINT: 1340 m

FAIRLY EASY

MID-JUNE TO END OF SEPTEMBER

START: From the junction of the Icefields Parkway and Hwy. 16 in Jasper, head west on Hwy. 16 for 11.1 km to a small unsigned parking area on the right (north) just after Meadow Creek Bridge.

DIFFICULTY: Easy walking on a well-established trail. Steep in places.

1. The trail starts on the railway service road. After 150 m climb the bank and cross the tracks at an X-ing sign and descend to the Miette River.

2. Cross the bridge and follow the trail (old wagon road) up the valley, then switchback and cross over a timbered ridge to the Minaga Creek drainage. Descend to the bridge over Minaga Creek.

3. About 400 m beyond the bridge over Minaga Creek you reach a junction. Keep right. The left-hand branch leads to Elysium Pass some 12 km away.

4. Hike gradually uphill for another kilometre to another junction. Follow the main trail straight ahead (#3e) to Dorothy Lake, the largest of the three lakes. Christine Lake, with its many little islands, is a short distance beyond Dorothy Lake. Follow a bushy trail along the shore to a good viewpoint near two islands.

5. Retrace your steps to the junction where a short side trail (#3f) leads left for 450 m to Virl Lake. This long, slender lake has views to Indian Ridge and Muhigan Mountain.

6. Return the way you came.

The Miette River from the bridge.

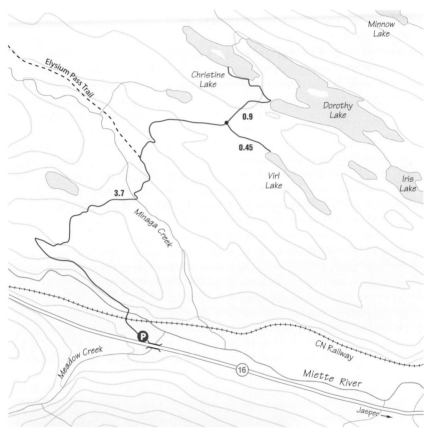

Minnow Lake

Elysium Pass Trail

Christine Lake

Dorothy Lake

0.9

0.45

Virl Lake

Iris Lake

3.7

Minaga Creek

CN Railway

P

Meadow Creek

16

Miette River

Jasper

LEFT: *Saskatoons in blossom. The berries provide food for foraging bears as well as chipmunks, squirrels and many woodland birds. Deer, elk and moose eat the leaves and twigs.*

OPPOSITE TOP: *Dorothy Lake.*

OPPOSITE MIDDLE: *Christine Lake.*

OPPOSITE BOTTOM: *Virl Lake with The Whistlers and Indian Ridge in the background.*

Contact Information

Banff National Park Information Centre
- 224 Banff Avenue, in the Town of Banff
- 403-762-1550
- pc.gc.ca/en/pn-np/ab/banff/visit

Lake Louise Visitor Centre
- Village of Lake Louise, next to Samson Mall
- 403-762-8421
- Trails office: 403-522-1264

Kootenay National Park Visitor Centre
- Located in Radium Hot Springs, B.C.
- 250.347.9505
- pc.gc.ca/en/pn-np/bc/kootenay

Kootenay Park Lodge Visitor Centre
- 68 km (45 minutes) north of Radium Hot Springs on Highway 93.
- 250-434-9648
- kootenayparklodge.com

Yoho National Park Visitor Centre
- Located at entrance to Town of Field
- 250-343-6783
- pc.gc.ca/en/pn-np/bc/yoho

Jasper National Park Information Centre
- Located about halfway along the main street in Jasper
- 780-852-6176
- Trails office: 780-852-6177
- pc.gc.ca/eng/pn-np/ab/jasper

Icefield Centre information desk
- Located at the Columbia Icefield
- 780-852-6288

Acknowledgements

Special thanks to my wife, Gillean, for the many photos not credited separately. You can tell which are hers: they are the best ones.

Emergency

Dial **911.**